Healed Wounds but Ugly Scars

Choices and Consequences

SAMUEL KORANTENG-PIPIM, PhD

BEREAN BOOKS
Ann Arbor, Michigan

An ADVENT PRESS Book
P. O. Box 0102, Osu, Accra, Ghana
Tel: +223 (21) 777 861 Fax: +223 (21) 775 327

Printed by Pacific Press, Nampa, Idaho 83687, USA

Published by Berean Books, Ann Arbor, Michigan, USA
Printed in the United States of America

First Printing, April 2009

Edited by Jerry D. Thomas
Cover Design by Gerald Lee Monks
Cover Resources from iStockphoto.com
Layout by Aaron Troia
Type Set in Adobe Garamond Pro 12/16

For your personal copy of *Healed Wounds, but Ugly Scars,* or for additional copies, contact your local Christian book store or mail your prepaid order ($14.99, plus $5.00 shipping and handling in the USA) to:
Berean Books, P. O. Box 2799, Ann Arbor, Michigan 48106, USA.
Website: www.berean-books.org

For quantity discounts to churches, schools, or groups, contact the author at the above address or at:
Phone: 734-528-2863; FAX: 734-528-2869; E-mail: skpipim@gmail.com.

Koranteng-Pipim, Samuel
Healed Wounds, But Ugly Scars: Choices and Consequences / Samuel Koranteng-Pipim

1. Choice–Religious Aspects—Christianity
2. Spirituality—Christian Life
3. Decision making—Religious aspects—Christianity
4. Forgiveness
I. Title

ISBN 13: 978-1-890014-11-7
ISBN 10: 1-890014-11-7

Dedication

To My Children

Ellen & Sam

Thank you for your gift to me. This is my gift to you.

Acknowledgments

This is perhaps the quickest book I have ever pulled together—all within two weeks! The urgency with which it was written was prompted by a number of factors.

Foremost among them was the pain of watching loved ones reap the consequences of wrong choices. This agonizing experience placed a heavy burden upon me to quickly assemble material that would speak passionately on the issue of choices and consequences.

I would also mention the role of Kingsley Osei, the General Manager of Advent Press in Ghana. He urged me to produce a work that would benefit both student canvassers and the general reading audience in West Africa. The deadline imposed by shipping schedules to Ghana was the external motivation that forced me to work within the two-week time frame.

As should be expected, writing this book involved many choices—including the unpleasant choices of sleepless nights and intrusion upon the valuable time of people who are near and dear to me.

I am particularly indebted to close friends, family, and the young people associated with CAMPUS. Their prompt feedback and valuable input at the different phases of the book's development steered me in the right direction.

Julia Chappelle-Thomas played a major role in smoothing and tweaking my first draft into clear, readable format. And she did it with speed and uncomplaining grace! I couldn't have asked for a more gifted person on this project.

It has also been a privilege working with the capable team at Pacific Press. Jerry Thomas, Dale Galusha, Aaron Troia, and Gerald Monks are the right combination of players to get work done in a timely fashion. Without their prompt responses and professional help, this work just could not have happened at this time. Thank you, Jerry, for planting the seed for the contents of this book.

Special thanks go to attendees and participants at various events where I initially presented the contents of this volume. Their positive testimonies confirmed to me that honesty and candor in addressing crucial issues are not only welcomed, but also greatly appreciated by serious young people and adults.

Most of all, I am greatly indebted to the Lord Jesus Christ for healing me of my own self-inflicted wounds. The visible—and not so visible—scars I carry today will forever remind me of His saving and sustaining grace. To Him be the glory!

Table of Contents

Introduction

A wound is an injury in which the skin, tissue, or an organ is damaged by some external force. An open wound results when the underlying tissue is torn, cut or punctured; a closed wound is where a blunt force trauma causes a contusion or bruise. When a wound is healed, it leaves behind a mark or a scar. Very serious wounds leave bigger or more prominent scars. No scar can ever be completely removed.

In this book, wounds and scars are used as metaphors for the consequences of wrong choices. Wounds refer to the consequences that are still fresh, and scars symbolize the lasting effects of past decisions and actions.

Every human being carries some scars. In our journey through life, we are often injured physically, emotionally, mentally, and spiritually. Some of the wounds that caused the scars are self-inflicted, whiles others were caused by other people. Even after we are healed, the scars still remain—and some of them are very ugly.

Scars tell stories, and the stories can be painful. They include lasting effects resulting from missed and neglected opportunities, broken hearts, failed relationships and marriages, painful betrayals and hurts, disappointing outcomes, and dashed hopes. The scars also expose the hidden experiences of rejection, fear, doubt, ruined health and finances, loss of innocence, shipwrecked faith, lifelong regrets, and more.

But although scars tell sad and tragic stories, scars don't bleed anymore. They don't have to bleed anymore. Scars are there to remind us that once fresh wounds are now healed. Rightly perceived, scars can inspire us to move on with our lives.

The primary purpose of this book is to help us avoid needless wounds—and the scars that result from them. In other words, the book is intended to caution against making wrong choices in our journey through life—choices that have far-reaching consequences upon ourselves and others. *Healed Wounds, But Ugly Scars* is also written to help us retrace our steps back to healing, after we have experienced the painful wounds of sin—either self-inflicted or caused by someone else. More importantly, the book is designed to lead us to the Wounded Healer, the One who alone can help us live with our ugly scars.

Healed Wounds, but Ugly Scars is the outgrowth of a series of sermons I preached to young people. Three of these sermons appear in Part I of this book under the sectional heading "Self-Inflicted Wounds." The first of these sermons, the title of which I have chosen for this book, was the opening address I gave in Sacramento, California at the 2004 convention of the Generation of Youth for Christ (GYC), a grassroots young peoples' movement in North America.[1]

The second sermon—"One Fatal Wound"—initially started out as one of five presentations I originally gave in 2006 to a group of students at Harvard University.[2] When I subsequently presented a revised version of the message in Minneapolis, Minnesota, during the 2007 GYC convention, I added a section which now appears as the third sermon in this book. It is titled "Avoiding Needless Wounds."[3]

The fourth sermon—"The Balm for Our Wounds"—is an adaptation from my book *Not For Sale: Integrity in A Culture of Silence,* a work that grew out of a 2008 sermon I presented to the Michigan Men of Faith and later to our CAMPUS missionaries at the University of Michigan.[4] The fifth major sermon contained in this volume—"Bleeding Scars"—has been preached on various university campuses under the title "For Jonathan's Sake."

Healed Wounds, but Ugly Scars also includes some valuable excerpts from the book—*Steps to Jesus*—a contemporary adaptation of the nineteenth-century devotional classic, *Steps to Christ.*[5] These excerpts have been included in this volume in response to frequent questions about what we should do after we've made some very bad choices. The selections appear in Part II of the present book.

Part III of the book concludes some thoughts on how to live with our ugly scars—the wounds resulting from both our self-inflicted wounds and the injury we have received from others. The chapters of Part III also contain the reflections of some public university students who were given the opportunity to read the manuscript and share their thoughts on the chapter titled "Scars of Love."[6]

The ultimate intent of *Healed Wounds, but Ugly Scars* is to assure readers that although we are all wounded, God wants to heal us. Only a Wounded Healer can offer complete healing. Only a Risen Savior with scars can understand our scarred hearts. Today, He is our Mediator in heaven, working to heal us of all our wounds:

For we do not have a high priest who is unable to sympathize with our weaknesses, but we have one who has been tempted in every way, just as we are—yet was without sin. "Let us then approach the throne of grace with confidence, so that we may receive mercy and find grace to help us in our time of need" (Hebrews 4:15-16; NIV).

The Risen Jesus, who once bid doubting Thomas to touch His scarred hands and believe (John 20:19-29), invites us today to come to Him with whatever scars we bear, with whatever wounds we carry, and with whatever doubts we harbor. He assures us that He will heal us of our ugly scars of life. These are the words of my favorite devotional author, E. G. White:

"The Elder Brother of our race is by the eternal throne. He looks upon every soul who is turning his face toward Him as the Savior. He knows by experience what are the weaknesses of humanity, what are our wants, and where lies the strength of our temptations; for He was in all points tempted like as we are, yet without sin. He is watching over you, trembling child of God. Are you tempted? He will deliver. Are you weak? He will strengthen. Are you ignorant? He will enlighten. *Are you wounded? He will heal.* The Lord 'telleth the number of the stars;' and yet 'He healeth the broken in heart, and bindeth up their wounds.' Ps. 147:4, 3. 'Come unto Me,' is His invitation. Whatever your anxieties and trials, spread out your case before the Lord. Your spirit will be braced for endurance. The way will be opened for you to disentangle yourself from embarrassment and difficulty. The weaker and more helpless you know yourself to be, the stronger will you become in His strength. The heavier your burdens, the more blessed the rest in casting them upon the Burden Bearer."[7]

The purpose of this book will be accomplished if *Healed Wounds, but Ugly Scars* succeeds in helping just one person to either avoid some self-inflicted wounds or find healing from such wounds—whether self-inflicted or caused by others—and live at peace with the ugly scars. I pray that many will be blessed by this work.

Samuel Koranteng-Pipim, PhD
Ann Arbor, April 2009

Endnotes

1. The sermon itself was inspired by a Bible study that was presented to our University of Michigan students by Randy Skeete, one of my colleagues at CAMPUS (Center for Adventist Ministry to Public University Students). I was so moved by his study that Tuesday night I just couldn't sleep that night when I got home. As I reflected on the many mistakes I and others had made in life, I decided to write a sermon for myself and the students I oversee. I subsequently presented that sermon at the 2004 Generation of Youth for Christ (GYC) meeting. For more on GYC, see www.gycweb.org.

2. At that time I titled the message "Why Continue On a Wrong Road, When a U-Turn Is Possible." I have since then presented that message with different emphases and under titles including, "The Urgency of Excellence" (at the University of Cape Coast, Ghana, February 2009), "The Fatal Consequences of Mediocrity" (at the Kwame Nkrumah University of Science and Technology, Kumasi, Ghana, February 2009), and "Why Make A Dumb Decision?" (to the Pan-African Club at Andrews University, Berrien Springs, Michigan, March 2009). It appears in this book as chapter 3—"One Fatal Wound."

3. The 2007 GYC session focused on what it means to be a real Christian. It was themed "BE"—shortened from "Be ye transformed . . ." (Rom 12:2). My seminar presentation was titled "Killer BE: The Enemy of Holiness."

4. Samuel Koranteng-Pipim, *Not for Sale: Integrity in A Culture of Silence* (Ann Arbor, Michigan: Berean Books, 2008), pp. 93-100.

5. The devotional classic, *Steps to Christ,* was originally published in 1892 by Fleming H. Revell Publishing, a company owned by a brother-in-law to Dwight L. Moody. It was the largest American publisher of religious books in the late nineteenth-century. *Steps to Christ* has since been published in about 150 languages, with well over tens of millions copies in circulation. The author of this life-changing masterpiece on successful Christian living, Ellen Gould White (1827-1915), is the most translated woman writer in the entire history of literature and the most translated American author of either gender, measured by the number of languages having at least one of her works. She came from a Methodist background and became one of the pioneers of the Seventh-day Adventist Church. Hereafter Ellen Gould White would be cited simply as "E.G. White." References to her works are from the standard editions, all of which are available either through Review and Herald Publishing (55 W. Oak Ridge Drive, Hagerstown, Maryland 21740; Phone 301-393-3000; www.rhpa.org) or through Pacific Press (1350 North Kings Road Nampa, ID 83687; Phone: 208-465-2500; www.pacificpress.com). In the USA and Canada, to find a local retailer near you call 1-800-765-6955. For more on E. G. White, see chapter 6, endnote 1 (pp. 110-111)

6. The students comprised of the eight 2008-2009 CAMPUS missionaries and some five students from Indiana University who had visited the missionaries during the latter's 2009 Spring break. Their names and reflections are found in chapter 13 of this book.

7. E. G. White, *The Desire of Ages,* p. 329; emphasis mine.

PART I

SELF-INFLICTED WOUNDS

(Making and Avoiding Wrong Choices)

"Nobody ever did, or ever will,
escape the consequences of his choice."
—*Alfred A. Montapert*

"Do not be deceived, God is not mocked; for whatever a man sows, that he will also reap" (Galatians 6:7).

"Turn your wounds into wisdom."
—*Oprah Winfrey*

Chapter 1
Wounds and Scars

"There is a way that seems right unto a man, but its end is the way of death" (Proverbs 16:25).

A sign at the crossroads in a southwestern state of the USA once read: "Be careful which road you choose—you'll be on it for the next 200 miles."

As on literal roads, the choices we make in the journey through life have far-reaching consequences. It is said that life is like a journey on a road. There are long and short roads, smooth and rocky roads, and crooked and straight roads. There are corners, detours, and crossroads branching off in many different directions. We must be careful about the choices we make on the road of life—for we shall be on it for a long time.

The journey through life consists of choices. And because choices do have consequences, both positive and negative, we must choose wisely.

The word consequence literally means "with a sequence," one thing following another or one thing resulting from another action or condition. Thus, certain things naturally follow what we think, choose, and do. The consequences can be far-reaching:

- Sow a thought, reap an action.
- Sow an action, reap a habit.
- Sow a habit, reap a character.
- Sow a character, reap a destiny.

The two great books of God—the book of nature and the Word of God—also illustrate how our decisions and actions have consequences.

Principles from the Two Books

There is an indisputable fact in nature: Harvest is determined by the sowing. If you want to harvest wheat, you must plant wheat. If you plant apples, you will not reap mangoes. We reap what we sow.

Just as the harvest in the realm of nature, the fruit of our lives is the corresponding outcome of what we have been planting and sowing in the choices we make. The Word of God sets forth this moral principle of life in this way:

> Do not be deceived, God is not mocked; for whatever a man sows, that he will also reap. For he who sows to his flesh will of the flesh reap corruption, but he who sows to the Spirit will of the Spirit reap everlasting life (Galatians 6:7, 8).

The above passage pictures human actions as seeds cast into the soil, bound by the same law that holds together the harvest and sowing in our fields. The decisions we make today affect our lives and that of others—both here and now and for all eternity.

The consequences of our choices seldom affect only us. Others will nearly always be affected—both now and in the future—by every decision we make.

For example, our career choices are not just important for today's job market. They can also have lasting effects upon our health, family, and our service to God. The decision we make about whom to marry will to a great extent determine our happiness in this life, and the happiness and emotional well-being of our children. In the same way, our choices of friends can bring blessings or curses.

Both human history and the Word of God record the examples of men and women whose choices—whether good or wrong—had some far-reaching consequences. And we shall do well to learn from the examples of others. This fact is remarkably illustrated in the life of one notable personality of the twentieth-century.

One Notable Example

William J. Blythe, III was born on August 19, 1946, in one of the poorest states in the United States. He was the only child of his mother. Three months before his birth, his father died in a tragic automobile accident. His mother later remarried and at the age of 14, William was legally adopted by his stepfather. For the remainder of his life, he bore the name of his adoptive father.

William had a difficult childhood, in part because his stepfather was a gambler and an alcoholic who regularly abused William's mother and, at times, his half-brother. But in spite of tremendous odds, he became one of the most influential people in the twentieth century. Though not always appreciated in his own nation, he is well respected and loved outside of his country. People overseas recognize him for his tremendous contribution to world peace and his concern for the needs of the poor and oppressed.

Early Years

In his early childhood years, he exhibited unusually solemn attitudes toward his religion. In the household of his mother, stepfather, and stepbrother, William was the only one who regularly attended church. William often walked to church alone. The church minister remembers that William was often waiting before he arrived to open up the church, and this was when William was only 13 years old. As a teenager, William continued to show the characteristics of someone much older.

As a teenager, William assumed the role of head of the household as his mother's marriage turned rocky. With an alcoholic stepfather that was often abusive toward his mother, William took it upon himself to create order. He hated to see the conflicts brought upon by his stepfather's alcoholism and so intervened multiple times to protect his mother and stepbrother.

These experiences had a significant impact on William's life and beliefs. William has always shown outstanding interpersonal skills, and he has often used those skills to create a consensus. Because of his desire to reduce conflicts, in his adult years William worked tirelessly for peace in the world.

The Scholar

Though from a very poor town, and though he studied in a small town high school, William excelled in his studies. He attended some of the most prestigious universities around the world. He earned a bachelor's degree in international affairs from Georgetown University in 1968, and he subsequently attended Oxford University on a Rhodes scholarship. He later earned a law degree from Yale University in 1973.

After law school, William returned to his home state and became a university law professor. He quickly became popular among the students because of his engaging teaching style. At a school new to desegregation, William helped black students who were still facing discrimination by other students and faculty members.

The Politician

In 1976, William was elected the Attorney General of his state at the age of 30. Two years later, he became the youngest governor in his country in over four decades as he presided over his state. In 1992 (at age 43), he became the President of the United States—the sole superpower of the world. He served two consecutive terms. During his presidency, his administration ushered in one of the most prosperous periods in America's history. His full name is William Jefferson Clinton. We know him as Bill Clinton.

But as I stated earlier, today Bill Clinton's contribution is not greatly appreciated—partly because of his self-inflicted wounds. His moral problems have tarnished his reputation and great accomplishments. Many Americans forgave Bill Clinton for his moral lapses. He survived an impeachment attempt that would have thrown him out of office. He served his full term. Yet, for the rest of his life, Bill Clinton has to live with, and suffer the painful consequences of, his wrong choice. Even the very mention of his name evokes some rather strong emotions in certain segments of American society.

Bill Clinton is not, however, alone in suffering from self-inflicted wounds—wounds people inflict upon themselves because of their own deliberate choices. In a real sense, all of us, like Bill Clinton, are suffering from self-inflicted wounds.

The Pains of Self-Inflicted Wounds

From Adam's day to our time, countless numbers of people have suffered needlessly through their own faults. You find them today in prisons, drug rehabilitation centers, in mental institutions, hospitals, homeless shelters, divorce recovery programs, on death row, and in well-kept graves.

They are all suffering from the painful consequences of sin. They are harvesting the fruits of their choices. You see, there is a basic law of nature: We reap what we sow. Sin has unavoidable consequences.

The question is this: Can it happen to righteous people? Yes.

While God forgives sins, it does not mean He removes the consequences. You had better believe this, because there is a new teaching floating around—even in our own church—which says, "Jesus will forgive you; therefore, you can do whatever you want." Ladies and gentlemen, while God forgives sin, He does not always remove the consequences.

- God forgives the sin of fornication (or pre-marital sex) and adultery, but He may leave the HIV-AIDS intact.
- He will forgive the smoker, but the smoker may suffer from damaged lungs.
- He forgives the drunkard but may not restore his liver.
- God forgives an abortion, but He may not restore a perforated or ruptured uterus.

What am I saying? Sin has unavoidable consequences. While God forgives sins, He does not always remove the consequences. Calvary's cross was the penalty for sin, but not necessarily for its consequences. Until Jesus comes again to make all things new, we shall often have to live with the painful consequences of our choices. *The wounds may be healed, but the ugly scars remain.*

The choices we make to sin inflict wounds upon us. The wounds are the consequences. Even when we are forgiven—even when the wounds are healed—the scars will still remain. In the words of my favorite devotional writer, "All who take part in that which dishonors God . . . *wound their own souls, and will carry the scars through their lifetime.*"[1]

This is why we have to be careful about the choices we make. To help you see this point, I am going to share stories of three Bible characters whose choices had some far-reaching consequences. The valuable lessons from their experiences will guide us in our own decision-making processes.

Endnote

1. E. G. White, *Review and Herald,* September 1, 1896, paragraph 13.

Chapter 2
Healed Wounds, But Ugly Scars

"Who is the most righteous person you can think of in the Bible?" To answer that question, many will suggest Noah, Abraham, Moses, David, Joseph, or other names. Few would ever mention the name Lot. Yet the Bible says that Lot was a righteous man.

Lot lost his father at an early age and was taken in by his uncle Abraham. Both he and his uncle Abraham became very wealthy; however, because of their combined wealth and a disagreement between their herdsmen, they were forced to separate. This was after Lot made a choice—a good choice, it seemed—until that one choice resulted in much sorrow and disgrace to this righteous man.[1]

A Righteous Man

2 Peter 2:6-8 tells us the story of the destruction of Sodom and Gomorrah. Notice how the Bible describes Lot:

> And turning the cities of Sodom and Gomorrah into ashes, condemned them to destruction, making them an example to those who afterward would live ungodly; and delivered righteous Lot, who was oppressed by the filthy conduct of the wicked (for that righteous man, dwelling among them, tormented his *righteous* soul from day to day by seeing and hearing their lawless deeds.)

Three times, Lot is referred to as a righteous man, yet few remember his story that way. We know he was a righteous man because, even though he lived in a wicked city, he was able to preserve his righteousness. In fact, the Bible says his righteous soul was stirred, it was vexed, whenever he saw sin around him.

Every one of us enjoys sin, but not righteous Lot. When (and I speak in a comparative sense), he saw some of the television programs of his day, his heart was pained. It's like a Christian working among people who are always cursing: it really hurts. When Lot visited the shopping malls and saw the magazines, his heart was pained. Something in him boiled when he listened to the music on the radio; his righteous soul was vexed. He was a righteous man.

We know he was a righteous man because he was able to rear two lovely girls who were virgins in an immoral city of Sodom. That takes a righteous man. It takes a lot of family worship—a lot of prayer to raise up such splendid girls.

We also know Lot was a righteous man because he had two older daughters who were properly married; they had their own husbands.

We know he was righteous because, at one time, when the angels visited and the people of Sodom wanted to sodomize them, out of desperation he was willing even to offer his best—his two daughters—to be abused by these Sodomites. Which father, in his right mind, would give his children to be abused? Righteous Lot—and the two virgin daughters—would rather suffer this kind of pain than cause innocent people to suffer.

He was a righteous man.

But do righteous people suffer needlessly for their silly mistakes? Yes. And the story of Lot tells us this. We find the account in Genesis 19.

Tragic Consequences

The Bible says a time came when Sodom was going to be destroyed, and God sent His angels with a message:

> Then the men said to Lot, "Have you anyone else here? Son-in-law, your sons, your daughters, and whomever you have in the city—take them out of this place! For we will destroy this place, because the outcry against them has grown great before the face of the LORD, and the LORD has sent us to destroy it." So Lot went out and spoke to his sons-in-law, who had married his daughters, and said, "Get up, get out of this place; for the LORD

will destroy this city!" But to his sons-in-law he seemed to be joking" (Genesis 19:12-14).

When he told them, "Get out!" his sons-in-law literally laughed in his face. They ridiculed that old man with his "superstitious fear." How could Sodom be destroyed? Its version of today's "homeland security" measures were impregnable. It had a powerful "anti-terrorist" squad. And of course, the popular preachers of Sodom assured everyone that a loving God will not destroy His children. For whatever reason, the sons-in-law mocked Brother Lot.

But Lot was not willing to give up. He was still concerned about the salvation of his sons-in-law and his two daughters. He pleaded with them. He would not leave right away. In fact, had it not been for the angels who literally dragged him out, he would have even lost his life. You read it from verse 15:

> When the morning dawned, the angels urged Lot to hurry, saying, "Arise, take your wife and your two daughters who are here, lest you be consumed in the punishment of the city." And while he lingered, the men took hold of his hand, his wife's hand, and the hands of his two daughters, the LORD being merciful to him, and they brought him out and set him outside the city" (Genesis 19:15-16).

Lot was delaying, and the angels had to drag him out in order to save him from the looming destruction. "The LORD being merciful to him . . . they brought him out and set him outside the city." Shortly thereafter the wicked cities were destroyed:

> Then the LORD rained brimstone and fire on Sodom and Gomorrah, from the LORD out of the heavens. So He overthrew those cities, all the plain, all the inhabitants of the cities, and what grew on the ground (24-25).

God destroyed *everything,* including Lot's business. But among the dead were his two married daughters and his two sons-in-law. Have you ever lost two brothers or sisters or two of your children in a day? Can you imagine attending such a funeral: the empty caskets and two freshly dug graves? That was the experience of Brother Lot. He lost all, overnight.

But there was more he lost. He also lost Mrs. Lot. When you read verse 26, the Bible says: "But his wife looked back behind him, and she became a pillar of salt." Lot lost everything because of his wrong choice. According to the book *Patriarchs and Prophets,* page 161, Lot's delay, his lingering, was partially responsible for the death of Mrs. Lot. It says:

> If Lot himself had manifested no *hesitancy* to obey the angels' warning, but had earnestly fled toward the mountains, without one word of pleading or remonstrance, his wife also would have made her escape. The influence of his example would have saved her from the sin that sealed her doom. But his hesitancy and delay caused her to lightly regard the divine warning.

Not only did Lot lose everything he had—his two children and sons-in-law—he lost Mrs. Lot. And for the remainder of his life, he had to live with the agony of knowing that his hesitation in leaving Sodom contributed to the loss of his wife. Any time he sat at the dinner table and saw salt, he remembered his wife and the role he played in losing her.

But there is another thing Brother Lot lost. The Bible tells us that Lot and his daughters went and dwelt in a cave. If you start reading verse 30, the Bible says: "Then Lot went up out of Zoar and dwelt in the mountains, and his two daughters were with him; for he was afraid to dwell in Zoar. And he and his two daughters dwelt in a cave."

Can you imagine a man who was used to city life suddenly reduced to living as a primitive caveman? Used to electricity and the latest gadgets of technology, suddenly he had to start life all over again—and all because of one foolish mistake we'll talk about in a moment.

But Lot lost more. If you keep reading from verse 31, the Bible tells us he lost his self-respect and, for the remainder of his life, he lived as a disgraced man. While they were hiding in the cave, Lot and his two cave daughters—those two virgin girls—well, the Bible tells us:

> Now the firstborn said to the younger, "Our father is old, and there is no man on the earth to come in to us as is the custom of all the earth. Come, let us make our father drink wine, and we will lie with him, that we may preserve the lineage of our father." So they made their father drink wine that night. And the firstborn went in and lay with her father, and he did not know when she lay down or when she arose.
>
> It happened on the next day that the firstborn said to the younger, "Indeed I lay with my father last night; let us make him drink wine tonight also, and you go in and lie with him, that we may preserve the lineage of our father." Then they made their father drink wine that night also. And the younger arose and lay with him, and he did not know when she lay down or when she arose.
>
> Thus both the daughters of Lot were with child by their father. The firstborn bore a son and called his name Moab; he is the father of the Moabites to this day. And the younger, she also bore a son and called his name Ben-Ammi; he is the father of the people of Ammon to this day (31-38).

While they were hiding in the cave, the seed that was sown in Sodom sprang up. These virgin girls discovered that there were no eligible young men in the entire area for them to marry, while their father, their righteous father, was growing old. He would soon die without a seed—no posterity—and they were concerned about the legacy of their father.

They could not stand the thought of living without husbands, so they did what the popular culture of their day had taught them. They mixed some wine in their father's juice (I'm trying to think how they did it), or perhaps they put it in his bread or cake, as sometimes happens on secular university campuses. They literally drugged their father and, in the language of today, they raped him.

They became pregnant. Nine months later, they bore children by their father. And Lot was known, in the entire area, as that hopeless man who fathered children by his own daughters. He lived a life of disgrace. Lot was reduced to living as a primitive caveman. He lost his wealth, his two married daughters, his sons-in-law, his wife and, ultimately, his self-respect.

But why? Why did Lot suffer so much? It was all because of one foolish choice he had made years earlier.

The Fatal Choice

When we flip our Bible back to Genesis 13, it tells us what happened when Lot was with his uncle Abraham. They had a large stock of cattle, and a fight erupted between the herdsmen of Abraham and the herdsmen of Lot. Abraham told him, "Look, we are brothers." Then:

> So Abram said to Lot, "Please let there be no strife between you and me, and between my herdsmen and your herdsmen; for we are brethren. Is not the whole land before you? Please separate from me. If you take the left, then I will go to the right; or, if you go to the right, then I will go to the left" (8, 9).

And what would Lot do? He was the younger, and he should have given the uncle the preference, but what did Brother Lot do? Righteous Lot?

> And Lot lifted up his eyes, and beheld all the plain of Jordan, that it was well watered everywhere, before the Lord destroyed Sodom and Gomorrah, even as the garden of the Lord, like the land of Egypt, as thou comest unto Zoar. Then Lot *chose* him [he made a choice] all the plain of Jordan; and Lot journeyed east: and they separated themselves the one from the other. Abram dwelled in the land of Canaan, and Lot dwelled in the cities of the plain, and pitched his tent *toward* Sodom (Genesis 13:10-12).

Lot made his choice. That one choice made on that location between Bethel and Ai was followed by another. He "pitched his tent *toward* Sodom." Abraham remained on that location, but righteous Lot started inching his way toward Sodom. "Why Sodom?" we may ask.

Sodom was a businessman's dream—a place of commerce and profit. All the banks and stock exchange brokerage companies were there. It was also a place for thc latest innovations and technologies. It had nearby the Ivy League educational institutions: Sodom State University and the University of Gomorrah, with their fantastic football and basketball teams. Sodom was a place of the future.

But like every business city, Sodom was likewise a place for pleasure. Like Sacramento, New York, or Chicago, Sodom was a popular tourist city and vacation spot. There were fun activities there. You can almost think of the Date Palm Parade, with its pounding music. There might have been the Olive Grove Beauty contest or, maybe, the Sodom and Gomorrah Annual Oscar Award nights, which paraded beautiful girls on the TV screens of Sodom (you should know by now that I'm actually talking about today).

Various musical stars were also in Sodom. They sang everything from heavy to soft rock, from rhythm and blues (R&B) to rap, hip hop, and gospel rock. Even the church in Sodom had its own brand of rock music that masqueraded in its style of contemporary worship as "praise worship."

And of course, there was sex: many different kinds of sex. Sex before marriage was not fornication—it was a relationship (have you noticed that the word "relationship" is neutral?). Sex outside of marriage was not adultery—it was an affair (it almost sounds neutral, as if you might be working in the ministry of foreign affairs). The promiscuous who were sleeping around were not promiscuous—they were just multi-friended.

There were different expressions of sexuality, from homosexuality to bisexuality and everything in between. Even the church in Sodom believed there was nothing wrong with homosexuality. They even ordained gay bishops in Sodom. Some in the legislative halls and ecclesiastical councils were even pushing for gay marriage in the enlightened cities of Sodom and Gomorrah (again, I'm talking about today).

You see, Sodom was not a place for Christians. But Lot, *righteous* Lot, "pitched his tent *toward* Sodom." He did not settle in downtown Sodom because it was too violent. He settled in the outskirts of Sodom, in the suburbs. But before long, the man who pitched his tent "*toward*" Sodom was living right inside Sodom. For instance, by the time you come to Genesis 14:12, the Bible tells us, "And they took Lot, Abram's brother's son, who dwelt *in* Sodom, and his goods, and departed."

The preposition has changed from *toward* to *in.* One little step led to another. After frequent trips into Sodom, Lot became convinced that he should move nearer the market. It would cut down on the cost of transportation in his business. He could sell his milk fresh; he could easily ship his wool. His business partners may have convinced him that in order to remain competitive, he should move his business to downtown Sodom.

I'm sure Mrs. Lot also convinced *righteous* Lot to move into Sodom. She would have all the latest bargains from the big stores in downtown Sodom; you don't get sales in the suburbs. And she could listen to the Sodom Symphony at Orchestra Hall in Sodom.

I want to believe that the two young virgin girls also convinced Dad to move to Sodom. They would be close to their older married sisters, and what was better to strengthen family values? Of course, these two girls did not like their small Jordan Valley Junior Academy. They wanted to attend the Twin-City High School. They needed to score well on the SAT scores so they could get scholarships to Sodom State University.

For whatever reason, Lot, righteous Lot—the man who had pitched his tent "*toward* Sodom"—found himself *in* downtown Sodom. In the city, he was living in a house. In fact, he was at the gate, and scholars suggest that he rose to be the mayor. From one seemingly innocuous choice on a location between Bethel and Ai, righteous Lot seems to be moving step-by-step towards his doom. From a great distance away, he moved *towards* Sodom, then found himself *in* Sodom, and now we see him *on top* of the pinnacle of Sodom's political power.

E. G. White says Lot owed his prosperity to Abraham, but instead of giving preference to his uncle in that choice, he was dazzled by visions of profit. Patriarchs and Prophets, page 133 says:

> Dazzled with visions of worldly gain, Lot overlooked the mor-

> al and spiritual evils that would be encountered there. The inhabitants of the plain were 'sinners before the Lord exceedingly;' but of this he was ignorant, or, knowing, gave it but little weight. He 'chose him all the plain of Jordan,' and 'pitched his tent toward Sodom.' [Notice the last sentence.] How little did he foresee the terrible results of that selfish choice!

Let me repeat the last sentence: *How little did he foresee the terrible results of that selfish choice!* What Lot did not foresee, he later saw very clearly:

- His business was gone.
- His married daughters were dead.
- His sons-in-law were dead.
- His wife was dead.
- He was reduced to living as a primitive caveman.
- His self-respect was gone.

Later, the Ammonites and the Moabites, the descendants of that incestual relationship, would become the enemies of Israel. We read again from *Patriarchs and Prophets,* page 167: "Lot's only posterity, the Moabites and Ammonites, were vile, idolatrous tribes, rebels against God and bitter enemies of His people."

Think about it. The legacy of this righteous man to the world was two rebellious nations—two nations that would always war against God's people. And all because of one foolish choice!

Throughout his life in Sodom, Lot had not been a happy man. Now he lived in a cave in shame. Was Lot's sin forgiven? Yes. Did he pay for the consequences of his wrong choice? Absolutely! *The self-inflicted wounds were healed, but the ugly scars remained.* Being righteous did not save him from the consequences of his wrong choice.

In fact, shortly after he moved into downtown Sodom, an invading army captured and looted all his possessions. His uncle Abraham risked his life to rescue him and his property. But after being rescued, Lot went straight back to Sodom (Genesis 14:8-12; cf. Chapter 19).

Had he not allowed selfishness to guide his life, Lot would have spared himself the suffering from these self-inflicted wounds. Notice what E.G. White says in *Patriarchs and Prophets,* page 168, talking about Lot:

> He was saved at last as 'a brand plucked out of the fire' (Zechariah 3:2), yet stripped of his possessions, bereaved of his wife and children, dwelling in caves, like the wild beasts, covered with infamy in his old age [that is, disgraced in his old age]; and he gave to the world, not a race of righteous men, but two idolatrous nations, at enmity with God and warring upon His people, until, their cup of iniquity being full, they were appointed to destruction. [Then notice the next sentence.] *How terrible were the results that followed one unwise step!*

Let me say it again. *How terrible were the results that followed one unwise step!*

Ladies and gentlemen, one unwise step is all it takes to reap some tragic consequences. The Bible furnishes us with many sobering examples.

One Unwise Step

Abraham made one unwise step in marrying Hagar, and now we are still battling with the war in the Middle East. One unwise step.

Adam and Eve thought it was just a simple fruit, yet it unleashed the radioactive fallout of sin into the whole world. One unwise step.

Esau thought it was just a little meal, and what's wrong with eating a little meal? He lost his birthright. One unwise step.

All these individuals and many more suffered the painful consequences of their unwise choices. *The wounds were healed, but the ugly scars remained.*

Brothers and sisters, we stand in great danger of repeating the mistakes of these Bible characters. Some of you started out as godly and splendid Christians. You used to study the Bible, pray, and attend Sabbath School. But somehow, you got off track. You went to college or started hanging out with the wrong crowd. All it took was that one unwise step, and you now find yourself in trouble.

One unwise step of skipping Sabbath School is all it takes: of not studying your Bible, of holding someone's hand in the dark and kissing, then more—one unwise step. Watching a particular movie or visiting a particular Internet site you know you shouldn't visit—one unwise step, and you lose it.

One unwise step of careless dressing and you will ruin yourself and trip up other people. Don't believe anyone who suggests to you that God has slackened His standards on Christian dress and adornment and that it is now OK to wear excessive make-up, flashing finger nails, and ornamental jewelry.[2] When such individuals tell you that you can dress casually and carelessly to church—they are putting you down. God will never lower His standards. What He has promised is that He will lift you up to meet the standard. Anyone who lowers the standard doesn't mean you well. One unwise step is all it takes.

One unwise step in an academic course, in a career choice, in a place to study or locate your business or home is all that it takes to ruin your life. Make no mistake, God is not mocked: Whatsoever someone sows, that, he or she will reap.

One unwise step in the choice of a friendship or one unwise step over lifestyle—even what and how you eat, the food you place on your plate, that little extra fat—and you will live for the remainder of your life working and sweating it out. One unwise step.

You can believe it. Ask around. You'll find stories of unhappiness and loss from those who made unwise choices. Somewhere along the line, they wanted to get married, and their parents told them, "Don't marry him/Don't marry her." They decided to go their own way, and now they are reaping the consequences of that foolish choice. One unwise step. One unwise attitude of rebellion and arrogance is all it takes.

Why am I saying this to you? We stand on the verge of the Second Coming of the Lord. And the Lord is waiting for a generation of young men and women who will dare to be all they can be and stand for truth, no matter the cost.

Whole institutions have been lost because of one foolish choice over who its leader should be—and or over the decisions by that one leader. Many local churches have been split apart and destroyed because of one foolish choice over music and worship style, setting young people off track. One foolish choice.[3]

Even as a worldwide church, we have had to live with the theological and hermeneutical consequences of certain pragmatic choices we have made over church racism, polygamy, divorce and remarriage, and women's ordination.[4] They each started with one unwise step.

I fear that we're still making some questionable choices in the way we want to grow our churches, do mission work, win and retain young people in the church, choose elders in our local churches, and who knows what other areas.[5] One unwise step after another.

Do choices have consequences? Do good and well-meaning people make foolish choices that can ruin lives—in their day and years and generations to come? Ask Lot!—righteous Lot. And he will tell you "Yes." Even when God forgives, even when the wounds are healed, the ugly scars remain.

If there are still doubts in your mind about the tragic consequences of sin, perhaps the following statements by E. G. White will help you see how the scars will still remain, even after one's wounds of sin are healed.

Healed Wounds, But Ugly Scars

"Common sins, however insignificant they may be regarded, will impair your moral sense, and extinguish the inward impression of the Spirit of God. All evil works ruin to those who commit it. *God may and will forgive the repenting sinner, but though forgiven, the soul is marred;* the power of the elevated thought possible to the unimpaired mind is destroyed. *Through all time the soul bears the scars.*"[6]

Do I need to say more? "God may and will forgive the repenting sinner, but though forgiven, the soul is marred. . . . Through all time the soul bears the scars." In other words, the wounds may be healed, but the ugly scars will remain—forever, through all time!

E. G. White is even more specific as she addresses different categories of people about the consequences of wrong choices:

To a businessman who was engaged in crooked business deals:

What did that dishonest man gain by his worldly policy? How high a price did he pay for his success? He has sacrificed his noble manhood and has started on the road that leads to perdition. He *may be converted;* he may see the wickedness of his injustice to his fellowmen—and, as far as possible, make restitution; *but the scars of a wounded conscience will ever remain.*[7]

To young people indulging in sensual gratification, here is a warning:

Any low gratification, any self-indulgence, is a scar left upon the soul, and the noble powers of mind are corrupted. *There may be repentance, but the soul is crippled, and will wear its scars through all time.* Jesus can wash away the sin but the soul has sustained a loss.[8]

To students in our institutions engaged in silly and trivial behavior:

I entreat the students in our schools to be sober-minded. The frivolity of the young is not pleasing to God . . . . Those who take the lead in these frivolities bring upon the cause a stain not easily effaced. *They wound their own souls, and will carry the scars through their lifetime.*[9]

And then, to unconverted ministers:

I call upon you who minister in sacred things to be converted men before you go forth to act any part in the cause of my Master. Now is your time to seek a preparation and readiness for the fearful test which is before us . . . . *Now it may be you can repent. But even if pardon is written against your names, you will sustain terrible loss; for the scars you have made upon your souls will remain.*[10]

I think the point is clear: Be careful of the choices you make. For they have far reaching consequences—both upon yourself and upon others—for all eternity. Wrong choices have some ugly consequences.

But the converse is also true. Right choices bring in their train positive results. When we do right, the Lord's presence abides with us. He not only blesses us, He also blesses all those within the spheres of our influence. This is what God did with Joseph when he maintained his integrity in the house of Potiphar:

> *The LORD was with Joseph,* and he was a successful man; and he was in the house of his master the Egyptian. And his master saw that *the LORD was with him* and that the LORD made all he did to prosper in his hand. So Joseph found favor in his sight, and served him. Then he made him overseer of his house, and all that he had he put under his authority. *So it was, from the time that he had made him overseer of his house and all that he had, that the LORD blessed the Egyptian's house for Joseph's sake; and the blessing of the LORD was on all that he had in the house and in the field.* . . . And the keeper of the prison committed to Joseph's hand all the prisoners who were in the prison; whatever they did there, it was his doing. The keeper of the prison did not look into anything that was under Joseph's authority, because *the LORD was with him; and whatever he did, the LORD made it prosper* (Genesis 39:2-4, 22-23).

In the light of what we've just studied, why not—at this very moment—make a commitment for right? Why not decide to follow the path of truth, integrity, humility, love, and faithfulness? These choices are possible if you know the Lord. Choosing Him is the wisest decision you can ever make.

Make the Right Choice—Today!

Of all the choices you will ever be called upon to make, the one that will affect your life more than any other is the choice to follow Jesus as your Savior and Lord. This one choice will have a bearing on every other choice you make in life—education, friendships and associations, career, marriage, recreation, who, where, when, and how you worship. Your decision to follow Him will also affect your outlook on life and how you deal with tragedies. More importantly, your choice for Jesus will determine your eternal destiny.

Why not make that choice right now? Simply tell Him you are sorry for your life of sin and how it has wounded you and many others. Ask Him to forgive you and give you the power to start living for Him. Believe that, through the power of His indwelling Spirit, He has given you all you need in your knew life of obedience to Him. Commit yourself to start studying His Word on a daily basis and communing with Him in prayer. And ask Him to make you willing to follow the path of truth that will be revealed in His Word. That's what it means to say "Yes" to Jesus.[11]

Do so now. For refusing to make even this choice is a choice. In case you are still hesitating, think about the following insightful quotes:

"When you have to make a choice and don't make it, that is in itself a choice." —*William James*

"Some persons are very decisive when it comes to avoiding decisions." —*Brendan Francis*

"Few people make a deliberate choice between good and evil; the choice is between what we want to do and what we ought to do."
—*E. C. McKenzie*

"Nobody ever did, or ever will, escape the consequences of his choice." —*Alfred A. Montapert*

"Choose for yourselves this day whom you will serve. . . But as for me and my house, we will serve the LORD." —*Joshua 24:15*

Endnotes

1. See Genesis 12, 14, & 19. This chapter is based on the opening address I gave in

Sacramento, California at the 2004 convention of the Generation of Youth for Christ (GYC), a grassroots young peoples' movement in North America. The sermon itself was inspired by a Bible study that was presented to our University of Michigan students by Randy Skeete, one of my colleagues at CAMPUS (Center for Adventist Ministry to Public University Students).

2. In 1 Timothy 2:9-10 and 1 Peter 3:1-5, the Bible (a) offers some general principles for Christian dress—namely, it should be modest, decent, and sensible; (b) prohibits the use of ornamental jewelry for adornment and extravagant or expensive clothes; (c) prescribes as mandatory the adornment of good deeds, humility, and submissiveness. The Old Testament passages below throw further light to the above New Testament passages: Isaiah 3:16-24 (wearing of jewelry, evidence of pride and apostasy—just as Peter said); Exodus 33:3-6 (Israelites told to take away their jewelry as evidence of their repentance); Genesis 35:1-4 (after his rededication to God, Jacob and his household took off their jewelry); Judges 8:22-26 (the reason the Midianites wore earrings was because they were Ishmaelites; this detail is important, showing that God's people were not Ishmaelites as to wear that type of jewelry). Hosea 2:13 (bodily ornamentation, evidence of apostasy); Lev 19:28 (avoid tattoos and other items of pagan adornment); Jeremiah 4:30, Ezekiel 23:40, and Hosea 2:13 (avoid the use of excessive make-up); Deuteronomy 22:5 (there should be clear gender differentiations in our clothing). The Scriptures teach that there should be a difference in the way believers and unbelievers dress. This is one reason why Revelation 12 and 17 contrasts the attire of two women, symbolic of God's true church and the apostate church.

3. For more on this see, Samuel Koranteng-Pipim, "Applause, Hand-Waiving, Drumming, and Dancing in the Church," Unpublished article on the author's website (www.drpipim.org). Visit, http://drpipim.org/index.php?option=com_content&task=view&id=108&Itemid=48

4. See my *Must We Be Silent: Issues Dividing Our Church* (Ann Arbor, MI: Berean Books, 2001).

5. Readers will be benefited by Samuel Koranteng-Pipim, ed., *Here We Stand: Evaluating New Trends in the Church* (Berrien Springs, MI: Adventists Affirm, 2005). It documents and responds to new teachings and practices that are making their way into our church, even as they are in other Christian denominations.

6. E. G. White, *Review and Herald,* December 8, 1891, paragraph 12; emphasis mine.

7. *Signs of the Times,* Feb. 7, 1884. Cf. *SDA Bible Commentary,* vol. 3, p. 1158; emphasis mine.

8. *Letters to Young Lovers,* p. 43; emphasis mine.

9. *Messages to Young People,* p. 382; cf. *Counsels to Parents, Teachers, and Students,* pp. 366-368; emphasis mine.

10. *Testimonies to Ministers,* p. 447; emphasis mine.

11. The chapters in Part II of this book will flesh out the summary above, giving you the specific steps that lead to a saving knowledge of Jesus Christ.

Chapter 3
One Fatal Wound

"How could it have happened?" This is often our reaction when we read shocking news of prominent people whose careers and lives have been ruined by some unforeseeable scandal. The scandal could be a moral indiscretion or financial embezzlement. It could involve illegal drug activity, a sudden divorce, pregnancy out of wedlock, contracting HIV AIDs, death, or some other consequences that seem irreversible.

The person caught in such a scandal could be someone you know and respect—your personal hero or heroine. That individual could be a trusted politician, a famous sports figure, a successful business executive, a beloved local church pastor, an outstanding professor, or a promising student who had everything going for him or her. That is, until that person's future is suddenly undone by a major catastrophe—often some spiritual, moral, or ethical failure.

When the highly esteemed people we know fall from grace, we almost invariably ask: "How could this have happened? What went wrong? Why did his or her life have to end up this way?"

How Could It Have Happened?

One doesn't have to read far into the Bible before asking those very same questions:

- How could Adam and Eve have exchanged their paradise home for a life of toil and death?
- How could righteous man Lot lose all his wealth, family, and self respect?
- How could King David have committed adultery with the wife of his trusted soldier and proceed to murder him to cover his crime?
- How could Miriam, the beautiful singer of Israel, have contracted leprosy?

- How could the apostle Peter—a prominent disciple of Christ—deny his Lord, and do so with an oath?
- How could Ananias and Saphira have died such tragic deaths when they seemed so sincere?

Important as these questions may be, we often ask them when it is too late. They are right questions at the wrong time. For ourselves, the time to ask those questions is not after we've experienced disgrace or ruin. We should ask—and answer—them *before* we ever face situations that lead to ethical failures or some other kinds of ruin.

For, you see, falling from grace seldom happens all at once. Most often, it is the culmination of a series of unwise steps. *We don't fall into sins, we crawl into them!*

The wounds we inflict upon ourselves and others are not accidents that just happen. If we pause to reflect, we will discover that they were bound to happen. They are the consequences of a series of previous choices we have made—wrong choices that could have been avoided.

So, what are steps that lead to destruction? What are the small compromises that often result in disaster?

This chapter will attempt to answer these questions by following the steps of a young man who inflicted upon himself a fatal wound, a wound that was needless and avoidable. It is the tragic story of a young man who thought he could toy with sin and get away with it. Unfortunately, he obtained the wages of sin—death.

Causes of Fatal Wounds

Although dangerous, sin is so enticing and so gripping that by the time it is encountered, it is already too late. Flirting with sin can be fatal. This is why the inspired Scriptures repeatedly urge us to flee from sin's temptation.

The story we're about to study is found in the book of Proverbs. This Bible book was largely written by Solomon, the wisest man who ever lived. You may know that Proverbs is a series of instructions about life given by a father as he prepares his son to become a responsible adult. In this book, the father tells his son *ahead of time* what to expect, what to cherish, and what to avoid. You may read this book as a manual on how to avoid needless wounds.

In Proverbs 7, the father explains to his son the anatomy of temptation—the dynamics of compromise, the steps that lead to destruction. To illustrate his point, the father describes a young man who gives in to the advances from a seductive woman and ends up being killed. The father begins his advice thus:

> My son, keep my words, and treasure my commands within you. Keep my commands and live, and my law as the apple of your eye. Bind them on your fingers; write them on the tablet of your heart. Say to wisdom, "You are my sister," and call understanding your nearest kin, that they may keep you from the immoral woman, from the seductress who flatters with her words (Proverbs 7:1-5).

Although Proverbs 7 is warning against seduction, the lessons from this passage go far beyond the topic of sexual immorality. The young man in the account we are about to study represents all of us: male and female, young and old. The advances from the seductive woman represent the allurements of sin's temptations. In this way, the instruction is a blueprint for dealing with temptations of all kinds—engaging in immoral sex and other ungratified desires, alcohol and drugs, dishonesty, and so many more.

The ten principles we shall extract from this account will be instructive in all situations.[1] They describe the common causes of our fatal wounds.

1. Being in the Wrong Crowd

> For at the window of my house I looked through my lattice, and saw among the simple, I perceived among the youths, a young man devoid of understanding (vv. 6-7).

"Tell me who you walk with, and I'll tell you who you are," so goes an old proverb. Our behavior is surely shaped by the people around us, and the company we keep shapes our characters more than we realize. These facts are remarkably portrayed in the passage under consideration.

When we first see this young man, he is in a crowd of people. But he is not just in any crowd, nor is he just any man. The passage says that this young man was found "among the simple" and "among the youths." You can tell the young man is in trouble because of the company he keeps: he is in a wrong crowd consisting of some naïve folks. "The simple" are the inexperienced, who are easily led astray (see Proverbs 1:4).

At this point, we must see that this metaphorical young man is really us: male and female, young and old, religious or non-religious. The first wrong thing that this man did was to place himself in the wrong crowd. One doesn't have to be a neurosurgeon to know that if you hang out with people who are drug dealers, party-goers, immoral, gossips, ungodly, lazy, etc., it will not take long before you start doing what the group does.

The company we keep and the things we behold in them do change us into their image. Because of the powerful effects of our environment on us and our character, we must be very intentional in where we go, who we see and spend time with, what we do, what we watch, what we listen to, etc. We are told: "Do not be deceived: 'Evil company corrupts good habits'" (1 Corinthians 15:33). Instead, we are urged to "assemble together" with people who will have positive influence upon us.[2]

Growing up in a religious home, the young man must have known the scriptural admonishment, "You shall not follow a crowd to do evil" (Exodus 23:2). Perhaps he reasoned that they were not going to do anything wrong. He was just hanging out with his friends; however, that is where his troubles began.

How is it with us? What crowds are we putting ourselves in? What do we watch? What do we read? Is sin given easy access to us through the environment created by the company with which we surround ourselves?

2. Lacking Common Sense

> . . . And saw among the simple, I perceived among the youths, a young man devoid of understanding (vv. 6-7).

Being in the wrong crowd is one thing, but being foolish is another. If you are grounded and sharp, you might take the opportunity to influence the crowd, to be a leader, to be an agent of change even in a group bent toward evil. Our young man was not one who could influence his crowd, for he is described as "devoid of understanding"—he lacked common sense!

The fact that the young man stood out as lacking common sense suggests that he wasn't just a naïve person like the other members of the wrong crowd; instead, he must have been *extraordinarily* naïve. He was probably one of the worst in the crowd! He may not have just been chronologically young; he was immature. He may be an older man in age, but still immature. He didn't have sense or discernment. He lacked judgment. He didn't know how to use his brains. To put it bluntly, he was stupid.

God has given us many tools to guide us through life, tools that ensure safety and holiness. One of these is our mind. We've been given the ability to reason through situations and discern danger. However, when we ignore reason, counsel, or common sense in a matter, we are setting ourselves up to fall.

We display a lack of common sense when we don't listen to sound advice from mature individuals or when we don't learn from the mistakes of others. We fail to use our minds when we don't make decisions ahead of time, but allow the circumstances to dictate what we do or don't do. We become situation ethicists.

The second step to moral, ethical, or spiritual downfall? Lacking common sense. Hanging in the wrong crowd and being stupid is a sure recipe for disaster.

3. Being At the Wrong Place

> . . . A young man devoid of understanding, *passing along the street near her corner; and he took the path to her house (v.8)*

Not only was the young man in the wrong crowd and without common sense, verse 8 tells us that he was also at the wrong place. Observe the movement of this young man. He initially seems only to be "passing along," then he draws "near her corner," and before long we find him taking the path "to her house."

At first, he did not take to the broad, open street. He sneaked about at corners, from where he could watch the woman's house without being observed by others. He sauntered slowly along, but before we are aware, he has taken a turn in the direction of her house. Notice that, thus far, it appears that whoever this new female character (the seductive woman) is, the young man is the one who is going out of his way to meet her.

It is when we make the *choice* to travel in forbidden territory that it becomes dangerous. When we fall into sin, it is because at some point in the process, we made an active, cooperative decision made to participate. It isn't sin that comes looking for us; in reality, the dangerous decisions that we make show that we are looking for sin.

We don't just fall into sins, we crawl into them. This young man made a choice to start heading towards the wrong place. Like Eve in the garden of Eden, the young man placed himself in forbidden territory. He was sauntering near the forbidden tree. Like righteous Lot who pitched his tent "toward Sodom," this naïve simpleton thought he could play around in a dangerous area without getting hurt.

Avoiding situations and environments where there is sure to be temptation is our best bet in not yielding to sin. For example, one of the ways alcoholics succeed in rehabilitation is by not walking into bars or stores that sell alcohol. They don't go to parties on the weekends, and they don't keep alcohol in their houses. This is because just being in a place where the temptation will be makes victory much less likely. Those areas are forbidden to them if they want to succeed.

Our forbidden territories may not be the bars. They could be surfing on particular internet websites, hanging out in certain internet chatrooms, visiting and consulting with psychics, going to gambling casinos, etc. . . .

4. At the Wrong Time

> . . . And he took the path to her house *in the twilight, in the evening, in the black and dark night (v. 9).*

What time of the day was the young man in that forbidden territory? Upon perusal of verse 9, it is clear that there is not just a list of times, but a sequence of times—"in the twilight, in the evening, in the black and dark night."

It starts out with the "twilight." Twilight is the soft, diffused light from the sky when the sun is below the horizon, either from daybreak to sunrise or, more commonly, from sunset to night fall. "Twilight" describes that invisible time within the 24-hour period when day turns to darkness (we call it dusk) or darkness turns to day (we call it dawn). It refers to that imperceptible fraction of nanoseconds when there is a change from one reality of time to the other. Since we know, in this verse, the "evening" comes right after "twilight," we conclude that the twilight aforementioned is dusk.

If we view twilight as the boundary between light and darkness, it becomes more interesting to note that when this young man made the decision to tread down a forbidden path, it was at the exact time of day when light began to turn into darkness. The symbolism is undeniable. This man made a very wrong decision but, also, at a very wrong time. How many times do we become more prone to sin because we make bad choices at deadly times?

It should also be observed that the young man was in the forbidden grounds *for a very long time*—from twilight, through the evening, to the night, till "the black and dark night"! The Hebrew expression for "the black and dark night" is literally, "in the pupil of the eye of night and in darkness." We have the same expression in Proverbs 20:20 to denote "deep darkness" or midnight. Its appropriateness is derived from the fact that the pupil of the eye is the dark center in the iris.

The young man was in forbidden territory for a very long time. He thought he could break the "curfew hours" of his parents' or school authorities' with impunity. He felt he could be in the beer bar or surf on the pornographic internet site for a long time without anything happening. He forgot that the longer you stay in forbidden territories, you more likely you are to make yourself prey.

You see, there are certain times in the day when we tend to be more vulnerable and when temptations tend to be more plentiful. Though we can sin and struggle at any time or point during the day, there is something about the covering of the night that assures those who would do wrong that no one can see and that they will get away with it. This is why we associate crimes and the wicked with darkness. Sin hates the light; it loves the darkness.

The point is we must stay away from the places, situations, and times where the natural thing would be to do something wrong. We must avoid settings where we are more prone to do the wrong thing.

5. Underestimating Impending Danger

> And there a woman met him, with the attire of a harlot, and a crafty heart. She was loud and rebellious, her feet would not stay at home. At times she was outside, at times in the open square, lurking at every corner (vv. 10-12).

"And there a woman met him." Where? "There"—on that forbidden ground. And it was also at the darkest part of the night when finally the seductive woman rears her head and comes out to meet this young man. Remember, in this parable, the woman represents the sins that tempt us, just as the young man represents all of us—male and female, young and old.

We must also point out that instead of surprising, or shocking, or jumping out at this young man, verse 10 says that this woman "met him." The young man saw her coming from a distance! Yet despite the impending doom, he just stood there until she arrived. He saw danger coming but chose not to do anything about it. He underestimated the impending danger, overestimating his own strength.

We know danger was coming because she is described as one "with the attire of a harlot, and a crafty heart." I can picture a woman with skimpy clothes, a dress that is slit half-way up the back or front to show a lot of skin. Most likely, she wore excessive make-up, flashy finger nails, and ornamental jewelry—the kind of dressing and adornment the Bible speaks against.[3]

This seductively dressed woman is also of a "crafty heart." She has a hidden agenda. She is crafty and secretive in her motives and intent. She's out to ensnare or trap the man. In other words, she was up to something—her agenda boldly advertised by how she dressed. The young man should have sensed danger approaching him. But he underestimated the danger, perhaps convincing himself that he could handle the situation.

As if, visually, her arrival was not noticeable, she was also "loud and rebellious" and "her feet would not stay at home." The description "loud" applies to a brute beast, stubborn and ungovernable, like an animal that will not bear the yoke (Hosea 4:16). So if somehow this young man could not see her, he could at least hear her coming. Even if he was blind, he was not deaf. The danger bells were ringing loud and clear. He could not plead ignorance of her arrival.

How often we do see sin approaching fast but do nothing? Instead of crying out to the Lord when we are in dangerous territories and asking for help, we place confidence in ourselves. Like the young man assuredly did, we think we can handle the situation. We grossly underestimate our capabilities to deal with sin.

It is worth noting that the last description of this woman mentioned is neither visual nor audible. When it says "her feet would not stay at home," we can deduce that this woman had a history. What the young man was going through with this woman had happened to others before. It is the same with us. We know that alcohol ruins people, immoral sex hurts relationships, and sin results in severe consequences. We've seen it over and over again, yet, somehow we think we can escape. We feel it will not happen to us. Sometimes we even say foolhardily, "I want to learn from my own mistakes—not from the mistakes of others." How self-deceived we can be!

You would think that the moment he saw the strange woman in skimpy clothes coming towards him in the dark, he would sense danger and walk the other way. But the young man shut his mind and downplayed how dangerous the situation had become. He still thought he was OK. He thought he could face the flirtatious woman and survive.

All too often, we ignore the warning signals of the dangers ahead. The alarming bells are ringing—poor grades at school, longer times with the

TV and internet, lessening of the time we pray, study our Bibles, go to Bible studies or church, etc.—yet we deafen our ears and shut our eyes.

We say to ourselves "I can handle it; No problem. I'll quit when I want." A little alcohol won't hurt. A little kiss, a little cheating, a little lie, a little . . . . But before we're aware, we are flat on our faces.

Temptations, like this seductive woman, are all around us—"not in the streets, now in the squares, lurking by every corner" (verse 12). We must always be aware of the dangers around: at work, at home, at school, in the church, everywhere— Satan like a roaring lion, is constantly prowling and seeking whomever it would devour. We must not flirt with danger.

6. Playing the Religious Game

> So she caught him and kissed him; with an impudent face she said to him: "I have peace offerings with me; today I have paid my vows. So I came out to meet you, diligently to seek your face, and I have found you (vv. 13-15).

From the moment she appears on the scene, the harlot takes control. Her appearance, her sounds, her past history and known attitude all scream danger. A stubborn woman who doesn't take "no" for an answer, she comes to meet him. Our simpleton stands no chance.

Her strategy is very simple. From the very beginning, she underscores the lustful nature of her errand. With a forceful kiss that stuns the youth, she proceeds to disarm whatever reservations he has by citing religious reasons. Already we can perceive the utterly hopeless and seemingly irreversible situation that this young man has put himself in. Verse 12 tells us that this woman, or rather sin, is now unabashedly visible and lurking in every corner, which means that there is no plausible way for this young man to escape this woman. He doesn't.

"So she caught him." This woman has launched a full frontal assault on this young man, and she does so with an "impudent" or bold, and unashamed face. She is no longer hiding her intentions. She is confident that she is able to seduce this young man. "So she caught him *and kissed him.*"

I can picture the young man literally frozen by the audacious move of the seductress. He's like a deer caught in the headlight, literally dazed or paralyzed. But the woman is clever and spares no time for this young man to hesitate. She disarms his shock with soothing religious assurances. She tells the young man that she has "peace offerings" with her and that she had "paid her vows" that very day. She assures him: "So I came out to meet you, diligently to seek your face, and I have found you."

Let's try to understand how she uses religious language to cover her seductive manipulation of this man. In the ancient worship of the Hebrew people, "peace or thank offerings" were divided between God, the priests, and the offerer. Part of the animal sacrifice was consumed by fire, the breast and right shoulder were allotted to the priests, and the rest of the animal belonged to the person who made the offering, who was to eat it with his household on the same day as a solemn ceremonial feast.[4] So when the seductive woman says that she has peace and thank offerings with her and that she has paid her vows, she is basically saying that she is a very religious woman.

I can hear her say to the young man, "Come on; loosen up! I don't mean any harm. I'm not as bad as you think. I am a very spiritual person. I am actually a Christian. I'm only kissing you with a holy kiss, just as the Bible says. We are brother and sister in Christ. In fact, I just came from prayer meeting at church. I've fasted about this encounter with you. You are an answer to prayer. In fact God has revealed to me—in a dream, vision, prophetic utterance—that I should be with you (or marry you)."

How many of these religious assertions do we employ as a cover-up for sin? Many times sin has so greatly disillusioned us that we use God and spirituality to hide it, and instead of killing the problem where the root is, we focus on polishing the external factors and allow sin to pervade our lives.

Often when we put ourselves in a situation that is dangerous, someone might do something that will shock us and cause us to think twice about what we are doing. I would imagine that this young man was shocked when the woman grabbed him and kissed him. But what we do after the initial shock defines whether we will continue the path towards destruction or start back up the path to righteousness and reconciliation. In many cases, deep down in our hearts we know that our tempters to sin are lying to us, but we choose to be deceived because we want to enjoy the sin.

Unfortunately, one of the ways that we get trapped is by deception done *in the name of religion.* As I've pointed out in my earlier work *Not for Sale,* religion often gives us the kind of justification we desire to continue our sinful actions.[5] Satan, the enemy of our souls, knows how to use religion to deceive. He tempted Christ in the wilderness using a religious pretext. Jesus warned about a religious deception in the last days. And the last book of the Bible makes it clear that the final issue in the last days that will engage the attention of the whole world will be religious in nature—we either worship God or worship the beast.[6]

When the seductive woman employed religion to hide her immoral advances, she was simply doing what many have all too often done—namely, she broke God's Law in the name of God.[7]

7. Succumbing to Flattery and Fantasy

> I have spread my bed with tapestry, colored coverings of Egyptian linen. I have perfumed my bed with myrrh, aloes, and cinnamon. Come, let us take our fill of love until morning; let us delight ourselves with love (vv. 16-18).

In addition to the religious game, the seductive woman now employs two of the most effective weapons in Satan's arsenal of flirtatious temptation: flattery and fantasy.

The word flatter means "to be smooth." Flattery is an act or instance of complimenting somebody, often excessively or insincerely, especially in order to get something. Flattery uses speech that may sound OK, but what is underneath is dangerous. As somebody has rightly observed, nearly every temptation has a little flattery in it, even if it's nothing more than the flattery of thinking you can "get away" with something.

Observe how the seductress begins by flattering the young man. Having found the man she had been praying for, she describes the expensive preparation she has made for exclusively the young man's entertainment—coverings of tapestry, Egyptian linen, bed perfumed with myrrh, aloes, and cinnamon. These imported items were very costly and much prized. They were luxury extravagances that kings and the wealthy would enjoy. Though harmless by themselves, what contaminates luxuries is the association with an illicit relationship and the rationalization of doing evil amid good, nice things.

The foolish young man finds himself suddenly treated as somebody. The seductress pumps up his ego by suggesting that he deserves to be treated as somebody very special—hence the expensive items. Perhaps no one had ever told him that he was Prince Charming, one who needed to be pampered. Now, his ego is stroked with the lavish plans made exclusively for him. Pure flattery! But he doesn't realize it because he is so foolish.

She doesn't just flatter him, she also leads him to a fantasy land. Fantasy is the creation of exaggerated mental images in response to an ungratified need. It is making you dream of that imaginary bliss that you would enjoy, if only you pursued a particular course of action—often a sinful action. Fantasy murmurs to us: Wouldn't it be wonderful if . . . ?

In this account, she refers to what they are about to do as drinking their "fill of love." But it's not love; it's wrong, immoral, and offensive to God. Through fantasy and flattery, the seductive woman appeals to his senses, much like sin causes us to fantasize to the point where our only desire becomes to fulfill those fantasies. She paints a picture of pleasure and delight through the immoral affair. And as we shall later discover, she was successful.

There is a reason why Hollywood constantly themes seduction and fantasy in their movies and shows. It hooks the viewer who lives vicariously through the people they were viewing. They fantasize or pretend it is them instead of actors. Satan knows humanity's weaknesses. He plays on insecure women who don't think they are beautiful by having men whisper sweet nothings in their ears. He plays on insecure men who don't believe in their own masculinity by having women affirm their strength and prowess. We must be careful not to let our desires lead us outside of God's plan for us.

Fantasy makes us think we are having a good time, when in actuality we are trapped. It reminds me of the story of a little boy who went fishing with his dad. As he observed schools of fishes swimming under the water, one of them caught his eye. He pointed it out to the father, saying: "Daddy, that fish is very happy; it is dancing." The father responded: "No son, it is not dancing; it is hooked. It appears it is dancing because it is trying to set itself free, but can't."

Flattery and fantasy gives us the illusion that we're dancing when we are actually hooked by the tempter. When we think about going to parties, drinking alcohol, using drugs, engaging in unethical and illegal activities, or even participating in some of the newly-minted worship contemporary worship styles, we may have the impression that we are having a good time. The truth is, we are hooked—heading towards the enemy's soup. That was the experience of the young man in Proverbs 7. He was made to believe that he was very special and the solicitations for "love" were designed for him to prove that he was a real man.

8. Rationalizing Away Sin and Its Consequences

> For my husband is not at home; he has gone on a long journey; he has taken a bag of money with him, and will come home on the appointed day" (vv. 19-20).

To put the icing on the cake, after appealing to his ego and fantasy, the seductive woman conjures up something for her victim's mind—rationalization. A rationalization is applying a good purpose to something that is inherently wrong. Rationalization makes us feel safe in sinning.

Observe how the seductive woman rationalizes away the sin they are about to commit and why it was safe for them to be sexually involved. It is evident that the woman is married, for she mentions her husband. She points out that her husband is not home; he has gone on a long journey, took money with him, and won't come back until a specific day. The message to the young man is that they will not be caught, and nobody will ever find out! There will be no consequences to the crime. It is safe to sin.

One reason we commit stupid mistakes—one reason why we often fall, inflicting upon ourselves some needless wounds—is that we try to convince ourselves that no one will know and that there will be no consequences for our choices and actions. Who in his or her right mind would speed in front of a police car? We do so when we think there will be no consequences. Of course, there are always consequences.

Just as in nature, so in the moral and ethical realm: We reap what we sow. There are always consequences for our choices and actions. There are police tickets, fines, and jails. We get expelled from schools, fired from jobs, and deported from foreign countries. Reputations are destroyed, marriages collapse, and presidents are impeached for betraying public trust. Other consequences to sin are unplanned pregnancies, HIV-AIDs, addiction to alcohol and drugs, and preventable deaths. We reap what we sow. Even if we don't receive the consequences in this life, it never escapes the notice of our Creator who will one day reward us all according to our deeds.

When we get into a situation that we know is wrong but we really desire to do what we want, we rationalize to make ourselves feel better. Rationalization pushes us right over the slippery slope that is so hard to come back from.

9. Willingly Sliding on the Slippery Slope

> With her enticing speech she caused him to yield, with her flattering lips she seduced him. Immediately he went after her, as an ox goes to the slaughter, or as a fool to the correction of the stocks (vv. 21-22).

I want to believe that even after the step of rationalization, the young man was still hesitant to do it. His conscience may have been bothering him still. But the seductive woman would not let him get away. For every possible objection the young man could have come up with, she responded with other justifications. "With her enticing speech" or "smooth words," she urged him on.

What happens next? Verse 22 says, "immediately he went after her."

It doesn't say that he takes some time to ponder the situation and let her know that, after thinking intelligently about it, he has decided he should follow her. The text says "immediately," or as some translations have it, "suddenly," or "quickly." Is this not our own experience? When it comes down to the final completion of the sinful act, we just rush ahead, like impulsive beasts, for our carnal nature has taken over and our minds and consciences no longer have any role in the process.

The adulterous woman in the parable, representing sin's temptations, is a relentless seductress. She flirts, flatters, and fantasizes with the first potential victim of her charms. "With her much fair speech she caused him to yield, with the flattering of her lips she forced him" (Prov. 7:21). She appeals to her victim's senses over and over again, drawing him in until he willingly goes to her.

After the step of "rationalization," the next step is almost a "no return." We slide along on that slippery slope. Even here, we must note that the choice is still ours. It is we who *choose* to follow the tempter. No one makes us sin; we choose to sin. It is we who *willingly* slide along the slippery slope to destruction. The will follows where the mind leads.

Despite her persistence, the woman is not the only one to blame for the young man's downfall. Indeed, he allowed himself to be taken in through a series of bad decisions. First, he spent time in the wrong crowd, among the simple (naïve, foolish). He also lacked common sense. He was at the wrong place, at the wrong time. He saw danger coming but foolishly chose to walk towards it. He allowed her religious game to weaken his resolve, as he yielded to flattery and fantasy.

The young man's last great mistake was to stand and listen to the woman's enticing words. And by the time it was over, he had wandered from the already spongy ground upon which he had been standing onto quicksand. Casting aside all scruples, he yielded to the temptation: "All at once he followed her like an ox going to the slaughter, like a deer stepping into a noose" (v. 22; NIV). Needless to say, he found himself on a strange bed "drinking his fill of love"—until the last chapter of his life was written.

10. Receiving the Fatal Wound

> Till an arrow struck his liver. As a bird hastens to the snare, he did not know it would cost his life (v. 23).

The young man follows the woman, as a fool or a criminal is led unresisting to the execution chamber. With a numbed conscience he drinks his "fill of love"—until "an arrow struck his liver."

Though the woman had assured him that they would be safe, they are not safe after all. The husband apparently returns unexpectedly and shoots an arrow straight into his liver—the seat of his lust. The deadly wound he receives is fatal.

We don't know what exactly happens to the young man. Perhaps the two of them are discovered and, for their crime of adultery, they are both stoned to death. But this much we know—there are many ways whereby sin exacts its ultimate price: gunshot, drug overdose, contracting sexually transmitted diseases or HIV AIDS, arrest, imprisonment, and execution.

That deadly arrow has fatally wounded so many people, confirming what the Word of God says: "There is a way that seems right to a man, but in the end it leads to death" (Proverbs 16:25). "The wages of sin is death" (Romans 6:23).

Sin has consequences. Those consequences may come in this life or in the next, but we can never escape the repercussions of our choices and actions. In the case of righteous Lot, we found out that it was a loss of his business, married children, wife, and his self-respect through his incestuous actions and a legacy of nations that warred against God's people. Though his wounds were healed, the ugly scars remained.

In the case of the young man of Proverbs 7, the wound is fatal. He dies a tragic and stupid death. Because it can happen to any of us, the Bible warns us: "Therefore let him who thinks he stands take heed lest he fall" (1 Corinthians 10:12).

Retracing the Steps of Destruction

Sin is bold and will thrust itself upon anyone—whether a righteous Lot or a foolish young man. Sin tries to cover itself with religion, fine accoutrements, pleasure, and comfort. Sin makes it seem like disobedience and illegal or unethical acts will work and that no one will know. When we follow sin's beckoning, they will always lead us to the chambers of death.

The passage concludes with an appeal to listen to counsel:

> Now therefore, listen to me, my children; pay attention to the words of my mouth: Do not let your heart turn aside to her ways, do not stray into her paths; for she has cast down many wounded, and all who were slain by her were strong men. Her house is the way to hell, descending to the chambers of death (vv. 24-27).

The example of the young man of Proverbs 7 shows us that we don't fall into sins—we crawl into them. Sin is not merely the completion of the act, but a process that begins the moment we lose faith in God and begin to trust in ourselves (Rom. 14:23). The young man didn't just sin when he slept with the seductive woman; he sinned the moment he began to leave the protection of God, wander into forbidden territory, and rely on his own wisdom and strength. And so he fell.

Sometimes our downfall begins when we consciously choose to turn those pages of a magazine or book, turn on and watch that television program, listen to that music, enter into that relationship, tell that small white lie, dress in a particular way, stop having our personal morning devotion or going to church, visit or hang out in that particular place, put that food item on our plates, or refuse to follow the Bible truth we have discovered.

What is the remedy against sin's powerful temptation? Listening to the counsel from the Word of God and the God of the Word:

> My son, keep my words, and treasure my commands within you. Keep my commands and live, and my law as the apple of your eye. Bind them on your fingers; write them on the tablet of your

heart. Say to wisdom, "You are my sister," and call understanding your nearest kin, that they may keep you from the immoral woman, from the seductress who flatters with her words (Proverbs 7:1-5).

Now we know why we often fall from grace. It seldom happens all at once. It is often the culmination of a series of unwise steps. They are the consequences of some unwise choices we make along the road of life—choices that could have been avoided. To save ourselves from fatal wounds, we must prayerfully study Proverbs 7 again and internalize it. This is what one of our young students has done in his poetic summary:

Hold fast to what I speak!
In my commands are life.
Let your gaze be illuminated by my law
Let it guide your hand.
Keep it that it may move your heart.
Join yourself to wisdom,
like a sister she uncovers the ways of the strange woman
counseling you against her flattery

I saw a young man, who surrounded himself with like-minded,
weak-minded men.
Not one to speak for reason.
I saw a young man walk in a way that flirts with destruction.
Walking between darkness and light,
he finds himself in black night.
In blindness he sees not the warning.
Like a venomous serpent her colors reveal the poison inside,
a subtle heart, cunningly devising destruction.
She moves out of her lair, and strikes with a kiss.
She allures him with pleasure and consoles him with piety.
"I've come with holy purpose,
"and my purpose purifies our pleasure.
"It is meant to be, else I would not have found you.

"We cannot refuse destiny."
Her bed, his grave, she has adorned in luxury.
Her sin stained sheets she has covered with fine linen.
Its foul odor, hid with the aroma of exotic perfume.
Sweet lips seduce with peace and comfort.
Subtle words betray her adultery.
"The Lord is gone, and his coming is far from us."
With fair words he is won to defilement.
Unthinkingly he rushes toward destruction,
Carelessly he binds himself in sin.
He swoops down for that which is sweet,
only to find himself entangled in death's embrace.

Will you not walk, O child, according to what I speak?
Do not let her move in your heart.
Wander not where she waits.
For the husk of many a man, even the mighty, still lie in her bed.
Their corpses mark the way to destruction.[8]

Indeed, sin does not only wound us and leave some ugly scars—sin would also kill us. The wounds of sin are fatal. To avoid crawling into sin, we must retrace the ten steps that led to destruction, learning some lessons along the way:

Step 1: Choose your friends wisely; avoid the wrong crowds.
Step 2: Be smart by preparing the mind ahead of time.
Step 3: Pick your locations wisely by avoiding forbidden grounds.
Step 4: Timing is everything; watch out for twilight and dark hours.
Step 5: Don't play dumb with fire; when you see danger coming, run as fast as you can.
Step 6: Beware of wolves in sheep's clothing—those who use religious language to deceive.
Step 7: Don't be pampered with the lies of flattery and fantasies.
Step 8: Never excuse sin and its consequences with rationalizations.

Step 9: Don't blunt your conscience by foolhardily plunging into sin.

Step 10: Remember that the wounds of sin are always fatal.

Endnotes

1. The message in this chapter was first presented as part of a 2006 Bible lecture series at Harvard University. It was titled at that time "Why Continue on A Wrong Road, When a U-Turn is Possible." I subsequently presented a revised version of the message at a 2007 GYC seminar under the title "Killer BE: The Enemy of Holiness." I'm indebted to the profound insights by our 2008-2009 CAMPUS missionaries: Dora Boateng, Michelle Lee, Jonathan Martin, Robert Mosher, Cassandra Papenfuse, David Park, Kayla Pina, and Brennen Vaneck. Their reflections on my devotional thoughts on Proverbs 7 during our "Principles of Ethics" class greatly enriched the contents of this chapter. I'm also indebted to Doug Sherman & William Hendricks, *Keeping Your Ethical Edge Sharp* (Colorado Springs, Colorado: NavPress, 1990), pp. 50-65, for framing the issues in Proverbs 7 in the larger context of ethical decision-making.

2. Hebrews 10:25; cf. 2 Corinthians 3:18.

3. In 1 Timothy 2:9-10 and 1 Peter 3:1-5, the Bible (a) offers some general principles for Christian dress—namely, it should be modest, decent, and sensible; (b) prohibits the use of ornamental jewelry for adornment and extravagant or expensive clothes; (c) prescribes as mandatory the adornment of good deeds, humility, and submissiveness. The Old Testament passages below throw further light to the above New Testament passages: Isaiah 3:16-24 (wearing of jewelry, evidence of pride and apostasy—just as Peter said); Exodus 33:3-6 (Israelites told to take away their jewelry as evidence of their repentance); Genesis 35:1-4 (after his rededication to God, Jacob and his household took off their jewelry); Judges 8:22-26 (the reason the Midianites wore earrings was because they were Ishmaelites; this detail is important, showing that God's people were not Ishmaelites as to wear that type of jewelry). Hosea 2:13 (bodily ornamentation, evidence of apostasy); Lev 19:28 (avoid tattoos and other items of pagan adornment); Jeremiah 4:30, Ezekiel 23:40, and Hosea 2:13 (avoid the use of excessive make-up); Deuteronomy 22:5 (there should be clear gender differentiations in our clothing). The Scriptures teach that there should be a difference in the way believers and unbelievers dress. This is one reason why Revelation 12 and 17 contrasts the attire of two women, symbolic of God's true church and the apostate church.

4. See Leviticus chapters 3 and 7.

5. Samuel Koranteng-Pipim, *Not for Sale: Integrity in A Culture of Silence* (Ann Arbor, Michigan: Berean Books, 2008) discusses the implications of how Jezebel and Ahab murdered principled Naboth by using religion as a ploy.

6. The Bible seems to point to this fact in Revelation chapters 12 to 14. For an insightful discussion of this prophecy, see C. Mervyn Maxwell, *God Cares: Volume 2, The Message of Revelation for You and Your Family,* pp. 309-419. See also Mark Finley, *The Next Superpower: Ancient Prophecies, Global Events, and Your Future* (Hagerstown, MD: Review and Herald, 2005), pp. 109–225. For an insightful discussion of the issues on religious liberty in the light of Bible prophecy, see Christa Reinach and Alan J. Reinach, eds. *Politics and*

Prophecy: The Battle for Religious Liberty and the Authentic Gospel (Nampa, Idaho: Pacific Press, 2007).

7. For example, the early Christian agape feasts were thus misused (1 Corinthians 11:20), and in modern times religious anniversaries (such as Christmas and Easter) have too often become occasions of immorality.

8. Robert Mosher, graduate of Michigan State University, and a 2008-2009 CAMPUS missionary.

Chapter 4
Avoiding Needless Wounds

In the chapter titled "One Fatal Wound," we traced the fatal steps of the foolish young man in Proverbs 7 as he walks into his death in the home of a married adulteress. From his tragic experience, we learned that we also are often most vulnerable to the fatal wounds of sin when we are in the wrong company, in the wrong place, and at the wrong time. The seductive temptress meets us with the kiss of death when we stroll to her house, falsely thinking we can escape.

But we don't always crawl into sin. Sin itself inches its way towards us. Sometimes, even after we take all the necessary precautions, the arrows of temptation search for us and try to assault us to leave their fatal wounds.

What should we do in such instances?

This chapter will address this question, by looking at the nature of temptations and how to overcome them. We will learn from the example of another young man who, unlike the foolish youth of Proverbs 7, makes all the right choices even though he faces some tremendous odds.[1]

Genesis 39 chronicles the account of Joseph, a young man who faces unbelievable temptation, yet prevails. More than any other, the classic story of Joseph in this chapter of the Bible presents one of the most valuable lessons in the Scriptures on how we can avoid the deadly wounds of sin.

Joseph comes through some very difficult circumstances and triumphs. We must point out, however, that unlike the young man in Proverbs 7 whose story is a parable, the account in Genesis 39 is a real historical event. Through the life of Joseph, we shall understand the nature of temptation and how to overcome it.

The Nature of Temptation

Temptation is an enticement to give in to our sinful desires, by doing what we know is wrong or displeasing to God. Temptation is not a sin. Yielding to it is. And when we give in to the lure of satisfying our sinful desires, it always leads to death. It inflicts fatal wounds:

> Let no one say when he is tempted, "I am tempted by God"; for God cannot be tempted by evil, nor does He Himself tempt anyone. But each one is tempted when he is drawn away by his own desires and enticed. Then, when desire has conceived, it gives birth to sin; and sin, when it is full-grown, brings forth death (James 2:13-15).

Temptation often comes unexpectedly. It arrives at familiar places—at our work place, at our home, at our school, and even at our church—when we are busy doing what we're supposed to do. This is what happens to Joseph, a godly and diligent Hebrew slave who has been brought down to Egypt, after having been previously sold by his own brothers to a caravan of Ishmaelite traders.

In Egypt, the Ishmaelite traders sell him to a man named Potiphar, the Captain of the Pharaoh's Guard. He is no doubt a powerful, wealthy military official in Pharaoh's army. Joseph is now about 17 or 18 years of age. He is diligent in his work for his new master Potiphar, even as he remains faithful to his heavenly Master, the God of the Hebrews. Joseph excels professionally and spiritually.

One day, as he is faithfully working in the house of his master Potiphar, temptation comes knocking at his door, sweetly whispering to him to commit adultery with his master's wife. From Joseph's encounter with the seductress, Mrs. Potiphar, we can glean some important facts about the nature of temptation and how to overcome it.

1. The Timing of Temptation

> And it came to pass after these things that his master's wife cast longing eyes on Joseph, and she said, "Lie with me." (Genesis 39:7).

Temptation sometimes strikes when we least expect it. Verse 7 states that Mrs. Potiphar cast her longing eyes upon Joseph "after these things." From the preceding six verses, we gather that "after these things" refers to a particular time when Joseph is enjoying maximum successes in every aspect of his life. Let's read the passage in its context:

> Now Joseph had been taken down to Egypt. And Potiphar, an officer of Pharaoh, captain of the guard, an Egyptian, bought him from the Ishmaelites who had taken him down there. The LORD was with Joseph, and he was a successful man; and he was in the house of his master the Egyptian. And his master saw that the LORD was with him and that the LORD made all he did to prosper in his hand. So Joseph found favor in his sight, and served him. Then he made him overseer of his house, and all that he had he put under his authority. So it was, from the time that he had made him overseer of his house and all that he had, that the LORD blessed the Egyptian's house for Joseph's sake; and the blessing of the LORD was on all that he had in the house and in the field. Thus he left all that he had in Joseph's hand, and he did not know what he had except for the bread which he ate. Now Joseph was handsome in form and appearance. And it came to pass after these things that his master's wife cast longing eyes on Joseph, and she said, "Lie with me" (Genesis 39:1-7).

It is evident that at the time temptation knocks on his door, Joseph is at the peak of his career. He is doing everything right and everything is going well with him. There are good reasons why Mrs. Potiphar casts her longing eyes upon Joseph. They are the same reasons any woman would be interested in a man:

- He is single and available.
- He is very spiritual (the Bible repeatedly says "The LORD was with him"; see verses 2, 3, 21, 23).
- He is a very successful young man. Everything he does prospers (vv. 2, 3, and 5).

- He is "handsome in form and appearance" (v. 6). In fact, only Moses, David, Saul, and Absalom in the whole Old Testament are described in the same manner.
- He is powerful and influential; he has oversight over the house of a prominent politician in Egypt (vv. 4, 6).

Which woman wouldn't be interested in such a young man? So when the Bible says that Mrs. Potiphar casts her longing eyes upon Joseph "after these things" (v. 7), it suggests that the temptation is timed for the most prosperous period of his life.

Sometimes we face our greatest temptations and trials during moments of our greatest successes, while we're doing very well in school, in our career, or in our spiritual lives. We must be careful when everything is going well for us, for that is often the time when temptation will strike. Just because things are going well in our spiritual and professional life doesn't mean we are entirely safe. Today's successes and victories often invite tomorrow's temptations and trials.

2. The Place of Temptation.

> And it came to pass after these things that his master's wife cast longing eyes on Joseph, and she said, "Lie with me." . . . But it happened about this time, *when Joseph went into the house to do his work,* and none of the men of the house was inside, that she caught him by his garment, saying, "Lie with me . . . "(Genesis 39:7, 11-12).

As mentioned earlier, temptation often arrives at familiar places: at our workplace, at our home, at our school, and even at our church, when we are busy doing what we're supposed to do. Unlike the foolish young man of Proverbs 7 who is obviously looking for trouble by "going near" the seductive woman's corner, Joseph is where he needs to be. He is not on any forbidden grounds. He is not doing the kinds of things that get us in trouble—hanging out with the wrong crowd, in places we have no business of being.

Joseph is simply at his duty, minding his own business. More importantly, he is exactly where God wants him to be. He is in a place doing what God wants him to do. He is doing what God could bless. Thus, "God was with him."

Sometimes we think that there will be no trouble when we're doing everything we know to be right. But that is not necessarily true. Often we are much more likely to be tempted or tried when things are going well for us. There are several reasons why our moments of success tend to be the time we often face our severest tests.

First, I want to believe that Satan tempts us during times of greatest successes in order to undermine our credibility and witness. Moreover, God sometimes allows the trials and temptations to test us when things are going well so that we are not filled with pride on account of our accomplishments or successes. For example, God permitted a "thorn in the flesh" of the apostle Paul, so that he wouldn't "be exalted above measure" (see 2 Corinthians 12:1-7, especially v. 7). The Lord doesn't want us to put trust in ourselves, but in Him. Furthermore, temptations and trials come our way during peaks of our successes in order to develop our character and prepare us for greater challenges and opportunities ahead.[2]

In any case, the place of Joseph's temptation is where he lives, works, and worships his God. Just as Mrs. Potiphar makes her sexual advances "when Joseph went into the house to do his work," so also will temptation often find us in our homes, workplaces, and churches—the places we're supposed to be.

3. The Instrument of Temptation

> And it came to pass after these things that *his master's wife* cast longing eyes on Joseph, and she said, "Lie with me" (Genesis 39:7).

In addition to the timing and place of temptation, there is also the "instrument of temptation"—the channel often employed to tempt us.

Satan can use any means and anyone to inflict fatal wounds upon us. In the story of Joseph, the enemy employs "his master's wife." We do not know her first name, but we know she is Mrs. Potiphar—the wife of Joseph's beloved master.

Unlike the young man in Proverbs 7, when Joseph faces his greatest temptation, it is not from a stranger but from one very familiar to him. The instrument of temptation is from within, and we're told, "We have far more to fear from within than from without."

The most effective means the enemy employs to trip us is through people we know. We can find them among our friends, family, classmates, co-workers, neighbors, and church members. They are often people we love and respect—our teachers, relatives, pastors, prayer-partners, choir-directors, professors, bosses, subordinates, neighbors—you name them.

In the account we're studying, we have a younger man and an older woman. She has power and influence over him, but he has the strength of character with him. She has the respect of age, position, wealth, and perhaps professional degrees, but he has integrity and God's truth on his side.

4. The Lure of Temptation

> And it came to pass after these things that his master's wife *cast longing eyes on Joseph,* and she said, *"Lie with me."* . . . But it happened about this time, when Joseph went into the house to do his work, and none of the men of the house was inside, that she caught him by his garment, saying, "Lie with me" (Genesis 39:7, 11-12).

For temptation to be temptation, it must come with some flattery and fantasy. It appeals to our carnal nature, enticing us to give in to our sinful desires. It invites us to do what we know is wrong or displeasing to God. In the case of Joseph, the lure of temptation is for him to sleep with the wife of his master, and it is the woman who casts her longing eyes and throws herself at him!

Mrs. Potiphar "cast longing eyes on Joseph." The literal Hebrew translation says that she "lifted up her eyes" at Joseph. *The Living Bible* says she "made eyes" at him. Whatever it is, we can be sure those looks are designed to tantalize and charm Joseph. We shouldn't even be surprised if she is dressed like the seductive women of Proverbs 7, Isaiah 3:16ff., and Revelation 17—instead of the modest women described in 2 Timothy 2, 2 Peter 3, Revelation 12.

One day she comes up to Joseph and says to him, "Lie with me." Mrs. Potiphar almost sounds like the seductive woman of Proverbs 7 who throws herself on the immature man, saying "let's drink our fill of love." You may remember her flattery and fantasy when she says, "you are a prayer answered, I've prepared for you with fine line, cinnamon . . . we shall not be caught."

Mrs. Potiphar is very much like a lot of rich, successful, and beautiful married women. They have everything, but are still not happy. Bored and unhappy with life, they try to find satisfaction in forbidden places—and they will offer anything to anyone who will want to please them. In the language of today, Mrs. Potiphar was a "single married woman." Her status as a married woman offered a convenient cover for her to live as a single woman. If Joseph was like any other man, her solicitation might be flattering to him.

Her offer must have been tempting to Joseph—as it would have been to many young men. Here he was, only a slave, yet his rich master's wife wanted to sleep with him. In my home country, Ghana, we call it a "free scholarship"—with many benefits (just as it would have been when a rich old man—a "sugar daddy"—throws himself on a younger woman). If Joseph responded favorably to the offer, he could have been treated really nice—no more as a slave, but as someone very special. He would have been a most fortunate man—very much loved by his master and now, if he gives in, also enjoying the special affection of his master's wife.

Such is the lure of temptation. It flatters us and makes us fantasize about the endless possibilities awaiting us if we will only yield to its enticements. It reminds me of how Satan used the same tactic on Eve in the garden of Eden. When he tempted Eve to eat the fruit from the forbidden tree, he told her she would not die, but rather be open-minded and achieve her full potential as God! He said to her: "You will not surely die.

For God knows that in the day you eat of it your eyes will be opened, and you will be like God, knowing good and evil" (Genesis 3:4, 5).

What is beckoning you to disobey God? What is trying to convince you that yielding to sin is advantageous? For Joseph, temptation's lure expresses itself when "his master's wife cast longing eyes" upon him and she said, "Lie with me." And it isn't just a one-time offer.

5. The Persistence of Temptation

> And it came to pass after these things that his master's wife cast longing eyes on Joseph, and she said, "Lie with me." But he refused . . . So it was, as *she spoke to Joseph day by day,* that he did not heed her, to lie with her or to be with her. But it happened about this time, when Joseph went into the house to do his work, and none of the men of the house was inside, that she caught him by his garment, saying, "Lie with me" (Genesis 39:7, 8, 10-12).

Mrs. Potiphar was not a woman who wouldl give up after Joseph said "No" to her initial advances. "She spoke to Joseph *day by day* . . . saying 'lie with me'." She was persistent. And such is the nature of temptation. It does not stop after we rebuff it the first time, or second time, or even the third time. It comes after us "day by day."

I've often wondered why Mrs. Potiphar kept coming after Joseph. Why doesn't she quit? Our students at the University of Michigan gave some insightful answers:

- "Maybe she felt humiliated by his initial rejection; she wanted to save face by succeeding."
- "Maybe she thought Joseph was playing 'hard to get,'" that he didn't mean it when he said "No."
- "Maybe he was initially scared—perhaps his master was only using her to test Joseph's integrity"; in other words, she thought he wanted to but was afraid to say "Yes."
- "Maybe she thought she could 'soften him up,'" perhaps she

thought she could wear down his resistance.

- "Maybe Joseph was shy, and needed a few more encouragements to 'come on'. Maybe next time he'd come around."
- "Maybe he thought people were watching—they would know—and would reveal the affair to his master."

Whatever the reason, she kept throwing herself at Joseph—"day by day." Sin is relentless. It never gives up. And so our resolve to stand firm against the lure of eating the forbidden fruit—any forbidden fruit—must also never surrender.

6. The Subtlety of Temptation

> But it happened about this time, when Joseph went into the house to do his work, and none of the men of the house was inside, that she caught him by his garment, saying, "Lie with me" (Genesis 39:11-12).

Not only is temptation persistent, it is also subtle. It devises cunning ways to wound its victims. It is sleek. It knows how to make the setting for sinning attractive. In the case of Joseph, it is evident that Mrs. Potiphar made sure her last desperate move would occur when no one was around. It is anyone's guess as to how no one was in that busy house on that eventful day.

Temptation always finds a way—a setting to make sinning very inviting. It creates—at least it attempts to create—an environment that makes us think no one is watching or that it is safe to sin. Such is the subtly of temptation.

7. The Boldness of Temptation

> But it happened about this time, when Joseph went into the house to do his work . . . that she caught him by his garment, saying, "Lie with me" (Genesis 39:11-12).

When we rebuff sin's subtle overtures, it becomes more brazen and more bold. Like the seductive woman in Proverbs 7 who forcefully "caught" the young foolish man and "kissed him," Mrs. Potiphar also caught Joseph. And with an impudent face, she brazenly said to him, "Sleep with me."

Mrs. Potiphar tried harder day-by-day. And as each time Joseph kept saying "No," she decided on a frontal assault. She is no longer coy or subtle. She is now daring and aggressive. (Reminds me of the enemies of Nehemiah—Tobiah, Sanballat, Geshem, and the Ashdodites; when subtlety didn't work they decided to openly attack Nehemiah; see Nehemiah 3 and 4).

Such is the nature of sin's temptation. When we repeatedly turn down its subtle and persistent advances, it becomes more desperate. Temptation is persistent and gains strength the more we resist; until, one day, it comes and forcibly grabs us. It literally seizes us and will not let us go until we yield.

The apostle Paul says in 1 Corinthians 10:13, "No temptation has *seized* you except what is common to man. And God is faithful; he will not let you be tempted beyond what you can bear. But when you are tempted, he will also provide a way out so that you can stand up under it."

Most men fall when temptation seizes them, as Mrs. Potiphar did to Joseph. But Joseph did not fall. How come? Why did he prevail? What lessons can we learn from him to overcome temptation? What choices can we also make?

II. Overcoming temptation

Although temptation kept knocking on Joseph's door, at each request Joseph's integrity prevails. Here's how the Bible puts it:

> And it came to pass after these things that his master's wife cast longing eyes on Joseph, and she said, "Lie with me." But he refused and said to his master's wife, "Look, my master does not know what is with me in the house, and he has committed all that he has to my hand. There is no one greater in this house than I, nor has he kept back anything from me but you, because you are his wife. How then can I do this great wickedness, and sin against God?" So it was, as she spoke to Joseph day by day, that he did not heed her, to lie with her or to be with her. But it happened about

> this time, when Joseph went into the house to do his work, and none of the men of the house was inside, that she caught him by his garment, saying, "Lie with me." But he left his garment in her hand, and fled and ran outside" (Genesis 39:7-12).

From this brief description we can flesh out some details about how Joseph handled Mrs. Potiphar's solicitations. The above passage is pregnant with principles on holding our ground and emerging unscathed from temptations. Among other things, it reveals the interplay of courtesy, clear-headedness, caution, courage, and faith as hallmarks of victory over temptation. Let's look at ten such principles.

1. Simply Refuse—Say "No"

> And it came to pass after these things that his master's wife cast longing eyes on Joseph, and she said, "Lie with me." But he refused . . . (vv. 7, 8).

How does Joseph handle temptation? The Bible says, he "refused," which means he simply says "No." The word "No" is the shortest word that travels the farthest. And when it is applied to any type of sin, the word "No" travels a very long way—even to eternity.

Though one doesn't have to learn complicated and confusing rules of grammar and syntax to say "No," it is the most difficult word to learn—especially when it comes to moral decision-making. Unlike Joseph, many of us could have come up with many excuses to not say "No":

- I didn't ask for it; she did.
- I am afraid of what she'd do if I say "No."
- I don't want to offend her.
- I'm simply following orders from my boss.
- We're both lonely—and alone.
- I'm only helping her; her husband doesn't have time for her, nor fulfill her needs.

- I'm sorry for her; I want to help her in her bad marriage situation.
- We're only human; we all have need for companionship.
- Everyone does it.
- We might as well do it because people may already think we're doing it.
- This is her best way of showing appreciation for my hard work.

Joseph has all these excuses to offer. But when sin makes its advances, saying "come and sleep with me," he simply refuses. He says "No."

How much we shall save ourselves from some deep wounds and ugly scars, if only we learn to say "No." Let's learn to say "No":

- When dared to indulge in a sinful act to "prove ourselves"
- When urged to cheat on an exam
- When tempted to lie about something
- When asked to give them our piece of mind
- When forced to pay them back for what they did to us
- When invited to keep quiet about our faith and principles
- When persuaded to hold on to tradition, instead of sound biblical teaching.

Saying "No" is the first step Joseph takes to avoid some needless wounds in the future. We must do likewise. We must say "No" to all options we know to be wrong.

2. Be Ready With Your Reasons—Know Why

> But he refused and said to his master's wife, "Look, my master does not know what is with me in the house, and he has committed all that he has to my hand. There is no one greater in this house than I, nor has he kept back anything from me but you, because you are his wife. How then can I do this great wickedness, and sin against God?" (vs. 8, 9)

A careful reflection on the passage indicates that Joseph doesn't say only "No" to her advances, but instead presents a sound moral argument as to *why* he cannot give in to the temptation to sin. He has a why for his "No."

Apparently, Joseph has thought through—ahead of time—his reasons for his beliefs and practices. He is not the kind of person who only has vague reasons for his views. He is one who can articulate his positions at a moment's notice because he knows his beliefs and the reasons behind them.

In the "Why Bible" lecture series I regularly conduct on various secular university campuses around the world, I always challenge my audience to know "why" they do what they do. I remind them that "He who knows *how* can get a job, but he who knows *why* will be the boss." A "know-how" is not as important as a "know-why." The one who knows "why" can handle any situation. In the words of German philosopher Friedrich Nietzsche, "He who knows *why* can bear any *how.*"

"Why" provides the reason behind our actions. Because our reasons often reveal our intentions and motivations, we must train our minds to give ready answers to whoever may ask us about our position or principles. The Bible says: ". . . always be prepared to give an answer to everyone who asks you to give the reason for the hope that you have. But do this with gentleness and respect" (1 Peter 3:15).

What to do in any given situation, and how to do it is always dependent on the *why.* We must know our reasons ahead of time.

Joseph made up his mind in advance. If he had waited until the time of temptation, it would have been too late. Daniel made up his mind ahead of time. He had purposed in his heart not to eat of the king's food (Daniel 1:8). Shadrach, Meshach and Abednego made up their mind in advance. They had decided ahead of time not to bow before Nebuchanezzer's golden image, no matter the cost (Daniel 3:16-18).

Observe, however, that it is not just important to say "No," and the reason for saying "No." We must also know *how* to say "No." The Bible says, "Always be prepared to give an answer to everyone who asks you to give the reason for the hope that you have. *But do this with gentleness and respect"* (1 Peter 3:15).

As Joseph "gently and respectfully" explains why he said "No" to his master's wife, he is courteous in *how* he did so. As we shall soon find out, each of his courteous "No" actions reveals an increasing determination, perhaps in proportion to the persistency of Mrs. Potiphar's "day by day" sexual advances.

3. Think of People's Trust In You

> But he refused and said to his master's wife, "Look, my master does not know what is with me in the house, and he has committed all that he has to my hand. There is no one greater in this house than I, nor has he kept back anything from me but you, because you are his wife. How then can I do this great wickedness, and sin against God?" (vs. 8, 9)

Joseph courteously reasoned on the basis of his master's trust. He cannot violate the trust reposed in him. How could he betray Potiphar who "has committed all that he has" to Joseph? How could he fail the one who had kept nothing back from him? Joseph understood the importance of trust. He comprehended that trust is like a flower vase; once it's broken, though you can fix it the vase, will never be same again.

One reason we easily yield to temptation is we forget the trust people have in us. In my own life I've discovered that one of the greatest inhibitors to sin is the realization that a lot of people trust me: my wife, children, relatives, friends, colleagues, students, church members, and employers. I know they'd be very hurt if I let them down. This realization has often spurred me on to do the right thing in many situations.

Without trust there can be no relationship—between us and others and between us and our God. This is why lying is such a big deal. It is not the fact that someone lies to you, but rather the fact that it makes it hard for you to believe him or her.

Abraham Lincoln was right when he said the following: "If you once forfeit the confidence of your fellow citizens, you can never regain their respect and esteem. It is true that you may fool all of the people some of the time; you can even fool some of the people all of the time; but you can't fool all of the people all of the time."

Joseph said "No" to Mrs. Potiphar's temptation by reasoning courteously on the basis of the trust of his master. In essence he was saying to her: "Even if I don't have—or care about—respect for myself, I care about the trust my master has in me. I cannot do him wrong. Too much is at stake in trust issues. I cannot let him down."

4. Think of God's Trust In You

> But he refused and said to his master's wife, . . . How then can I do this great wickedness, and sin against God?" (v. 8)

Joseph reasoned on the basis of God's trust in him. Yes, sin harms us because there are consequences for those who sin. Indeed, sin damages the trust people have in us. But above all, sin is against God, for it violates His holy law and character. It betrays the trust relationship between us and God. For these reasons, Joseph asked: "How then can I do this great wickedness, and sin against God?"

In asking this rhetorical question, Joseph was undoubtedly reflecting on how God has been good to him. It was He who shielded this Hebrew lad from harm, when his own brothers plotted to kill him. It was the Lord who made him prosper in Egypt. This God had always been, and was always with, Joseph. Though unseen to mortal eyes, the God who was with him was watching his every action and would be very hurt if he betrayed His trust. More importantly, Joseph knew that he belonged to God. He could not sleep with another person's wife because such an act was displeasing to his Lord.

In Joseph's response, I hear the echo of the words of Polycarp (ca. 69 – ca. 155), a second century bishop of Smyrna. At 86 years of age, this old man was arrested, condemned, and brutally put to death because he would not renounce Jesus Christ as Lord and because he would not worship Caesar as Lord. When Polycarp was urged by the proconsul who said, "Swear, and I will set thee at liberty, reproach Christ," Polycarp responded with these famous words, "Eighty and six years have I served Him, and He never did me any injury: how then can I blaspheme my King and my Savior?"[3]

Like Polycarp, Joseph refused to betray God's trust. He did not fall prey to the advances of his boss's wife; he recognized that if he yielded, he would not merely be wronging the woman and her husband. He would not just be violating his own conscience and tarnishing his own reputation. He understood that sin is against God.

We can save ourselves from many the needless wounds of sin if, at the time of temptation, we remember that more than people's trust in us, God trusts us and expects us to stand firm. If we don't care about another's trust in us, at least let's consider how good God has been to us. Like Joseph, let's remember God's blessings upon us in the past—His mercies and deliverance from death in a pit into which his brothers had placed him, protection on the long journey, favor in Egypt, etc. (see verses 2-5). Let's also consider God's special plans for our life. Can we throw all that away because of one sin? Can we betray God's trust in us?

To sleep with Potiphar's wife would certainly have been a sin against Potiphar, who had entrusted everything he owned to Joseph's care. But Joseph understood that a higher trust was at stake. He could not commit adultery because it was a sin against God. It was a betrayal of the trust relationship that existed between himself and his God.

Every sin we commit breaks our relationship with God. When Eve ate the fruit from the Tree of the Knowledge of Good and Evil, she sinned against God. When Cain murdered his brother Abel, he sinned against God. When King David committed adultery with Bathsheba and killed her husband Uriah, he sinned against God. When Ananias and Saphira lied about their assets, they sinned against God. When the church—your church and mine—rejected sound biblical teaching for tradition and cultural expediency, it sinned against God. When we don't worship God on His appointed holy day and in His prescribed way, we sin against God.

Every sin we commit breaks God's heart. This is why Joseph reasoned courteously for why he said "No" to the sexual advances of his master's wife.

5. Call Sin By It's Right Name

> There is no one greater in this house than I, nor has he kept back anything from me but you, because you are his wife. *How then can I do this great wickedness, and sin against God?*" (v. 9).

When Joseph asked, "How then can I do this great wickedness, and sin against God?", he called the advances of Mrs. Potiphar by their right name—sin. They were an invitation to commit adultery. One reason why we often fail or fall spiritually is that we try to rationalize away sin or disobedience. Not so, however, with Joseph. He knew that adultery was wrong. He called it "a wicked thing" and a "sin against God." He did not try to make sin less sinful by renaming it.

Today, the words "adultery" and "fornication" are too judgmental, so we prefer words like "affair," "relationship," "tryst," "fling," "hook up," and "one-night stand." We even call it "making love." But Joseph understands that adultery by any name is still adultery. Or as someone said, renaming sin doesn't change its character any more than calling rat poison food turns it into bread.[4]

Joseph called sin by its right name. He was a model of what the world needs today. In the words of E. G. White, my favorite devotional writer,

> The greatest want of the world is the want of men—men who will not be bought or sold, men who in their inmost souls are true and honest, *men who do not fear to call sin by its right name,* men whose conscience is as true to duty as the needle to the pole, men who will stand for the right though the heavens fall.[5]

Perhaps it will not be out of place for me to make some parenthetical observations about the disappearance of sin in our religious, ethical, and cultural discourse. Very few would question the assertion that today sin is airbrushed from our vocabulary and consciousness. In 1973, the Christian Psychologist Karl Menninger lamented this fact in his book entitled, *Whatever Became of Sin?*

As should be expected, the fallout from this downgrading of sin is incalculable. Some ugly old-fashioned sins are getting a face lift, wearing new pretty clothes and taking respectable seats in the church. I don't need to be specific for readers to understand that once forbidden and frowned-upon sins are baptized and ordained in our churches—in the name of compassion, justice, equality, inclusiveness, balance, diversity, or some other self-defined concepts. Even the twin ugly sins of greed and pride have come to church as "prosperity gospel" and "self-esteem ministries," respectively.

As sin disappears from our vocabulary and consciousness, it should also come as no surprise that the solution to what used to be called sin is now sought in self-help programs, self-esteem and positive thinking, therapy, meditation, or counseling. Repentance has been replaced by acceptance, and being happy is now the substitute for being holy.

Furthermore, our "don't judge me" culture does not always appreciate those who speak the truth or who call a spade a spade. George Orwell (1903-1950) was right when he said, "In an age of universal deceit, telling the truth is a revolutionary act." To which I'd add, "In a culture of theological pluralism, biblical teaching is controversial and divisive."

The disappearance of sin from our vocabulary today is a symptom of the ethical crisis of our time. The crisis is not in the flagrant violation of morally accepted standards of behavior (every age has had its share of this). Rather today's ethical crisis has to do with the fact that "for the first time, at least on a mass scale, the very possibility of such [moral] standards has been thrown into question, and with it, all essential distinctions between right and wrong."[6]

In other words, today's ethical crisis stems from the fact that, unlike in previous times when people knew what was right and wrong but chose to practice the wrong, in our time people are not entirely sure of whether there are universal moral absolutes to define what is right and wrong. We live in a culture of moral *relativism*.

Against this tidal wave of moral relativism and ethical entropy, God calls upon His people today to proclaim and uphold his Moral Ten

Commandment Law as the only unchanging and unchangeable law in the universe (not physical laws, which can be transcended by God). This Law is the only unerring standard of right and wrong.[7]

Joseph called sin by its rightful name. He rightly identified Mrs. Potiphar's offer "a wicked thing." And he rightly asked, "How could I . . . sin against God?" Because he understood that it was sin, Joseph knew exactly what to do.

6. Don't Entertain or Listen to the Source of Temptation

> So it was, as she spoke to Joseph day by day, that *he did not heed her,* to lie with her or to be with her (v. 10).

Just as he had "refused" or said "No" during the first instance of Mrs. Potiphar's sexual advances, so he did in subsequent instances. "As she spoke to Joseph day by day, that he did not heed her." In effect, Joseph refused to listen to what his master's wife was saying.

With the persistence of Mrs. Potiphar, Joseph realized that "gently and respectfully" explaining why he said "No" was not enough to ward off his master's wife. His courtesy did not mean he lacked backbone. With resolute conviction, Joseph told the temptress: "If you don't respect what I've already explained to you—the trust of others and of God, and the fact that adultery is sin and wickedness—I don't want to listen to you on this issue anymore!"

There come moments when we must simply refuse to entertain certain subjects. When tempted to talk about or listen to some compromising discussions, we must have the courage of our convictions to cut off such discussions. We must not listen to any such things AGAIN.

Don't only say "No." Say "No more." Don't ever pay attention to the source of our temptation. Cut off any *conversations* or suggestions in that regard. Period. Don't listen. Mother Eve got into trouble when she tried to have a conversation with the Enemy. Don't entertain the source of your temptation. Be bold in affirming "No." But more importantly, don't worry about whether or not her feelings will be hurt when you tell her plainly that you prefer the subject never be raised again in your presence.

Besides courtesy, not listening or entertaining your Mrs. Potiphar is a necessary caution against falling into sin. But there's more you can do.

7. Cut Off All Contact

> So it was, as she spoke to Joseph day by day, that he did not heed her, to lie with her *or to be with her* (v. 10).

Not only would Joseph "not heed her, to lie with her," the Bible also tells us that Joseph will not "be with her." He does not listen *to* her and he is not *with* her. In other words, Joseph takes additional precautionary measures by avoiding one-to-one contact with her.

If somebody is tempting you to sin, like Joseph, cut off all communications: no phone contact, e-mails, or letters. Don't even receive calls. When that person's caller ID flashes on your mobile phone, don't answer the ring. Don't reply to any e-mails and letters—don't even open emails and letters from this person. Delete the emails from your inbox and shred the letters. Period.

To not "be with" the source of your temptation also means that you must determine, by God's grace, not to allow yourself to be in situations where you could be tempted to sin emotionally, mentally, or physically. For example, you may decide not to have meetings alone behind closed doors with the opposite sex. Don't drive in the same car alone. If you have to be with that person because of professional or spiritual reasons, get a third person to accompany you.

If the source of your temptation is not a person, you must resolve not to expose yourself to it. For example it may mean that you should not allow entertainment or other influences that put sin (immorality, lust, murder, lies, etc.) in a favorable light or to fuel unholy desires. Don't visit certain websites or chat rooms. Don't read certain books or magazines. (Remember, when you are reading, you are keeping company *with* the source of your temptation).

8. Flee—Run for Your Life!

> But it happened about this time . . . that she caught him by his garment, saying, "Lie with me." But he left his garment in her hand, and fled and ran outside" (Genesis 39:11-12).

Paraphrasing Ecclesiastes 3, the words of the wisest man who ever lived (King Solomon), to everything there is a season. There is a time to talk and a time to stop talking. There is to be courteous and a time to be cautious. There's a time to dialogue and a time to draw the line. There's a time to listen and a time to not listen. There's also a time to stay and a time to go. This latter point translates for Joseph as a time to flee.

When Mrs. Potiphar physically threw herself on him one day, he didn't hang around to discuss the situation with her; he acted instantly and decisively—*he fled!* Whenever the New Testament dwells on the subject of sensual temptation, it gives us one command: FLEE! We are to RUN for our lives! We must get out of there! The apostle Paul may have been thinking of Joseph when he wrote to the Corinthian believers to "flee fornication" (1 Corinthians 6:18). He also instructed Timothy, a young minister to "*flee* also youthful lusts" (2 Timothy 2:22).

Fleeing doesn't mean you're chickening out. It simply means you are smart enough to know when danger bells are ringing. And if that means leaving behind your garments, so be it. When your house is on fire, there is no time to worry about your clothes. You may even run out in your underwear to save your life. Sometimes your salvation from a burning house may require fleeing naked.

Joseph fled, leaving his garment in Mrs. Potiphar's hands. He was willing to sacrifice something dear and personal to him. He was willing to keep his integrity, even if that meant running out without his clothes.

For us, fleeing may mean making every effort to relocate, transfer, change jobs, or change rooms. Consider the following practical suggestions by one of my favorite contemporary Christian authors:[8]

- If *overeating* is a problem to you, you may plan not to be there at that potluck nor visit that tempting restaurant. Or ask a friend or family members to hold you accountable for what you eat at that event and when. You may even deny your flesh by fasting on that day or periodically.
- If *alcohol* or *drugs* are your problem, you may have to stay away from bars; or liquor stores don't hangout with people who drink.
- If you are hooked on *computer games,* causing you to waste God's time, you may need to give them up completely.
- If you are enticed by *pornography* or lured into *unhealthy relationships over the Internet,* you may want to put your computer in the family room where everyone can see the screen, decide not to use the computer when you are alone or at night. If necessary, get ride of your Internet service or satellite or cable service.
- If *romantic movies* make you discontent with your singleness or dissatisfied with your husband or wife, or if they fuel sexual fantasies in your mind, don't watch them.
- If *certain magazines* plant unholy thoughts or desires or images in your mind, drop your subscription to the magazines, or toss the books.
- If you're being drawn into an *illegitimate relationship with a co-worker—or counselor or doctor you are seeing*—get out! Request transfer, quit your job, cancel your next appointment, find a biblical counselor/doctor of the same sex, or ask a married couple to counsel you.
- If you're tempted to be *physically intimate* with the person you're dating, don't single date. If necessary, take your sister or friend or your mother with you! If you've already violated biblical standards of purity in the relationship, you probably need to break it off completely.

These radical steps are what "fleeing" may mean. They may hurt, but if you want to please God, this is what it may entail. This is what Jesus means when he says, "If your right hand causes you to sin, cut it off and throw it away" (Matthew 5:30).

Sometimes we find it very difficult to let go of certain sins. We think we'll be miserable without them. The truth, however, is that those very things we hang on to will keep us from the joy we desire. Those tempting sins will enslave us and cause misery. Responding to those of us who think it is too much of a sacrifice to give up certain sinful ways, E. G. White writes:

> But what do we give up, when we give all? A sin-polluted heart, for Jesus to purify, to cleanse by His own blood, and to save by His matchless love. And yet men think it hard to give up all! I am ashamed to hear it spoken of, ashamed to write it.
>
> God does not require us to give up anything that it is for our best interest to retain. In all that He does, He has the well-being of His children in view. Would that all who have not chosen Christ might realize that He has something vastly better to offer them than they are seeking for themselves. Man is doing the greatest injury and injustice to his own soul when he thinks and acts contrary to the will of God. No real joy can be found in the path forbidden by Him who knows what is best and who plans for the good of His creatures. The path of transgression is the path of misery and destruction.[9]

If we want to avoid the fatal wounds of sin, we must always have a plan—an exit plan—to escape from tricky situations. Having such a plan does not indicate that you expect to sin. It is precautionary. Fire extinguishers and exit routes are put in buildings as precautions. We don't wait till our house is on fire before looking for fire extinguishers or exit routes.

If we are to "flee" the grip of temptation, we must have an exit plan. The good news is that we don't have to reinvent such a plan in our spiritual battles. The Bible says, "There hath no temptation taken you but such as is common to man: but God is faithful, who will not suffer [allow] you to be tempted above that ye are able; *but will with the temptation also make a way to escape,* that ye may be able to bear it" (1 Corinthians 10:13).

The Word of God is a critical component in the exit plan for the

Christian. David wrote: "How can a young man cleanse his way? By taking heed according to Your word. . . . Your word I have hidden in my heart, That I might not sin against You" (Psalm 119:9, 11). But the most comprehensive components of our spiritual exit plan are found the Christian armor (Ephesians 6:10-20). That is the way of escape—the way to flee—from the grip of Satan's temptation.

9. Be Willing to Pay a Price for Principle

> And so it was, when she saw that he had left his garment in her hand and fled outside, that she called to the men of her house and spoke to them, saying, "See, he has brought in to us a Hebrew to mock us. He came in to me to lie with me, and I cried out with a loud voice. And it happened, when he heard that I lifted my voice and cried out, that he left his garment with me, and fled and went outside."
>
> So she kept his garment with her until his master came home. Then she spoke to him with words like these, saying, "The Hebrew servant whom you brought to us came in to me to mock me; so it happened, as I lifted my voice and cried out, that he left his garment with me and fled outside."
>
> So it was, when his master heard the words which his wife spoke to him, saying, "Your servant did to me after this manner," that his anger was aroused. Then Joseph's master took him and put him into the prison, a place where the king's prisoners were confined. And he was there in the prison (Genesis 39:13-20).

Joseph paid a dear price for being true to principle. He was accused of attempted rape, and exhibit A was in the hand of the accuser—his coat. Exhibit B was the fact that he was nowhere to be found when she cried out for help. We may even hear echoes of racism in Mrs. Potiphar's words when she calls him "a Hebrew." It doesn't take a racist jury to find Joseph guilty. For the rest of his life he would have to live with that criminal record—at least in the minds of some.

Another price Joseph paid was an unjust imprisonment. He was thrown in jail among other common criminals. For the rest of his life, he would carry a label as an ex-convict. We know Joseph was hurt because, later in his life, after years of being in jail, he told one inmate about how he felt:

> But remember me when it is well with you, and please show kindness to me; make mention of me to Pharaoh, and get me out of this [prison] house. For indeed I was stolen away from the land of the Hebrews; and also I have done nothing here that they should put me into the dungeon" (Genesis 40:14-15; emphasis mine).

Loyalty to God is sometimes costly—most times. "Yes, and all who desire to live godly in Christ Jesus will suffer persecution" (2 Timothy 3:12). Our Lord Jesus Himself paid dearly—with His life—for living a sinless life.

We should, therefore, not be surprised that we have to pay a price—sometimes a costly price—for being true to principle. There is ridicule, loss of education and career opportunities, ruined reputation, misrepresentation, false accusations, and attacks from false brethren.

But if it hurts to do right, it hurts more to do wrong. It really hurts to live with a guilty conscience and suffer the consequences of our wrong decisions and actions. Another way of putting the price of loyalty into perspective is this: Obedience to God hurts, but disobedience also hurts (as we learned too well from the stories of Lot and the young man of Proverbs 7). So, if it costs us something to either obey or disobey, the real issue is: for which are you willing to pay a price?

One reason we inflict wounds upon ourselves is that we are not willing to make costly choices. So we compromise on things we know to be right. The apostle Peter gives us the two choices and explains why we must be willing to pay the price of faithfulness or loyalty to Christ:

> For what credit is it if, when you are beaten for your faults, you take it patiently? But when you do good and suffer, if you take it patiently, this is commendable before God. For to this you were

> called, because Christ also suffered for us, leaving us an example, that you should follow His steps: " Who committed no sin, nor was deceit found in His mouth"; who, when He was reviled, did not revile in return; when He suffered, He did not threaten, but committed Himself to Him who judges righteously; who Himself bore our sins in His own body on the tree, that we, having died to sins, might live for righteousness—by whose stripes you were healed. For you were like sheep going astray, but have now returned to the Shepherd and Overseer of your souls (1 Peter 2:20-25).

Joseph avoids wounding his soul (his spiritual relationship with God) by choosing, rather, to suffer the consequences of doing right. The world may see him as an attempted rapist and a criminal worthy of imprisonment. But His God is with him—even going to jail with him.

10. Trust God's Providence, Even When He seems Absent

> But the LORD was with Joseph and showed him mercy, and He gave him favor in the sight of the keeper of the prison. And the keeper of the prison committed to Joseph's hand all the prisoners who were in the prison; whatever they did there, it was his doing. The keeper of the prison did not look into anything that was under Joseph's authority,[a] because the LORD was with him; and whatever he did, the LORD made it prosper (Genesis 39:13-23).

Though it initially appeared that God had forsaken Joseph, abandoning him to the injustice of the system, God knew what He was doing. He was with Joseph in prison, granting him favor with the prison authorities. Eventually, through a series of circumstances we call divine providence or divine appointments, Joseph left the jail to become second-in-command in Egypt.

The experience of Joseph confirms the biblical teaching of divine providence. What this means is that God has a plan for the lives of His children. Divine providence affirms that circumstances—good and bad—are tools God uses to shape and mold and fit His children for their purpose and destiny in life. The apostle Paul expresses the doctrine of divine providence in the following words: "And we know that *all things* work together for good to them that love God, to them who are the called according to his purpose" (Romans 8:28).

"All things"—not "some things" or even "most things," but all things—work together for good. That little word *all* captures the scope of God's promise. I know that sometimes, under certain circumstances, it is hard for us to take God at his Word that *all* things will actually work together for good. But the apostle Paul made it very clear that "all things" include every inconvenience of life— the disappointments, sorrows, illness, pain, poverty, hardships, broken hearts, slander, and everything else we find awful.

In verses 35, 38, and 39 of Romans 8, Paul lists some of the things included in the *all things:* tribulation, distress, persecution, famine, nakedness, peril, sword, death, life, angels, principalities, powers, things present, things to come, height, depth, and "any other creature" that will attempt to separate us from the love of God. All these will work together for the good of God's children.

The Romans 8:28 passage is not suggesting that all things are good in themselves. We know that some things are bad and evil. What the apostle Paul is suggesting is that God can take even bad things and make them for the eternal good of His children. He brings good from evil, patience from suffering, sympathy from pain, and humility from disappointment.

This truth is best seen in the life of Joseph. Through his brothers' rejection and betrayal, his subsequent enslavement in Egypt, accusation by Mrs. Potiphar, and wrongful imprisonment, Joseph eventually was able to say to those who had hurt him, "You meant evil against me; but God meant it for good" (Genesis 50:20).

Trusting God's providence is one of the most powerful motivations to do right, no matter the cost. We must therefore say "No" to sin's temptations, even if our decision initially hurts. Ultimately, God will use our circumstances to accomplish His will for our lives.

Ultimate Secret of Victory

There is one phrase that keeps showing up in Genesis 39, the narrative about Joseph: "The LORD was with him" (verses 2,3,21,23). I want to believe that this is the secret to avoiding and prevailing over temptation. There are three implications arising from the knowledge of God's presence with Joseph.

First, there is no inherent power in Joseph, no inherent goodness. All his righteousness was like a filthy rag (Isaiah 64:6). He prevailed over the many temptations that had come his way because "the Lord was with him." It was an act of grace alone. God's grace and power were at work within him. Joseph's secret was not in himself—for self cannot conquer self. To depend on self is to head for defeat.

Joseph's reply to Mrs. Potiphar revealed his ultimate secret: "How . . . can I do this great wickedness, and sin against *God?*" That was the answer right there: looking away from himself to God. This God was "with him," and because God's presence was with Joseph, he prevailed over difficult temptations.

Second, God's presence with Joseph suggests that the only way to resist and overcome sin and temptation is to avail ourselves of the resources God has provided. They include the following:[10]

- Meditation upon the Word of God
- Prayer
- Sharing our faith
- Loving obedience to His will

Finally, the knowledge that "the LORD was with him" strongly affirmed that God had a plan for the life of Joseph and all things were under His control to work for His child's good. This fact ultimately gave him the motivation to say to Mrs. Potiphar, "How then can I do this great wickedness, and sin against God?" (Genesis 39:9).

The knowledge of God's providence—God's purpose and plan for us—frees us from the fear that often leads to compromises to sin. It greatly strengthens a person's resolve to go all the way for the Lord. One Christian author who has clearly and forcefully presented this biblical teaching is Carlyle B. Haynes, the author of the best-selling classic *God Sent A Man:*[11]

> Let a man believe that, and apply it to every circumstance of life, and it will result in the cultivation of his spiritual nature, the culture and development of his spiritual mind. There will come to that man great thoughts and a wide-open understanding of God's purposes, a far-reaching vision and timely adjustment to sudden setbacks and sudden promotions. That man will go steadily, inexorably forward in the way God has marked out for him to take, and to the places for which God has prepared for him.
>
> No accident can happen to such a man. Things do not happen to him by chance. He is God's man, God's agent, and everything that occurs to him comes to him through the hand of God.
>
> Nothing can really hurt such a man. His feelings can be hurt, he can be plunged into terrible grief, he can be shocked by the hatred of brethren; but these things work together to his real good as he believes God and yields to His disciplining hand.
>
> The greatest fact in the universe is the existence of God. God is. Each individual is dealing with an invisible Person who controls the universe and has a plan for his life.
>
> The second greatest fact of the universe is the will of God. God has a will and all things are under control of that will. That will has marked out a plan for my life.
>
> Just to believe these two facts equips a man to live, equips him for success, equips him for achievement, equips him to accomplish the will of God. Get everything else you can, but with all your getting do not fail to get these fundamental truths.
>
> Joseph believed God; he knew God; he loved God; he followed God; he trusted God. That was Joseph's essential preparation for life, the sum total of his education. It was quite enough.
>
> An education without God is an incomplete and inadequate education, even for this life. Just to know God and believe Him, to love Him and to follow Him, is adequate for success similar to Joseph's.

I invite you to develop, by the grace of the Lord, a rock-bound faith in God Himself, to take Him as your counsel, to look upon Him as your friend, to believe that He has a plan and purpose for you to fulfill, confidently to expect Him to bring you at last into the place of serve and final happiness that will identify you with His people through the ages to come.

Endnotes

1. This chapter amplifies a presentation I gave at a seminar in Minneapolis, Minnesota, during the 2007 GYC convention. The theme for that seminar was titled "Biblical Holiness: A Guide To Sinners." In the course of my presentation—titled "Killer BE: The Enemy of Holiness"—I used Joseph's story in Genesis 39 to talk about how we can avoid and overcome temptation. It is that presentation that I have expanded in this chapter of *Healed Wounds, but Ugly Scars.*

2. For more on why God sometimes permits trials and afflictions, see my *Patience in the Midst of Trials and Afflictions* (Ann Arbor, Michigan: Berean Books, 2003).

3. So great was the dismay and sorrow occasioned by Polycarp's maryrdom that the church at Smyrna recorded it in detail in a letter sent to the church at Philomelium, 200 miles to the east. This came to be circulated among the churches, generally. Such stories stirred Christians to hold the line in times of persecution. The church historian Eusebius copied most of the Martyrdom into his *Church History,* 4.15. The account of Polycarp's martyrdom gives us an insight into how the early Christians were persecuted, and it may also shed some light on Revelation 2:8-11, Christ's letter to the church of Smyrna (the very city where Polycarp was a Bishop).

4. Haddon Robinson, "God Still Expects Sexual Purity," *Good News Broadcaster,* May 1996, p. 35.

5. E. G. White, *Education,* p. 57; emphasis mine

6. Will Herberg, "What is the Moral Crisis of Our Time?" *Intercollegiate Review* (Fall 1986):9.

7. See, Ecclesiastes 12:13, 14; Matthew 5: 17-19; John 14:15 James 2:8-12.

8. Nancy Leigh DeMoss, *Holiness: The Heart God Purifies* (Chicago: Moody Press, 2005), pp. 117-121; emphasis mine. For more than 25 years, Nancy has communicated her burden for both personal and corporate revival and spirituality in conferences and retreats throughout North America and abroad. She is the host and teacher for Revive Our Hearts, a nationally syndicated radio program for women. She is also the general editor of Biblical Womanhood in the Home. For more information, visit her website: www.ReviveOurHearts.com.

9. E. G. White, *Steps to Christ,* p. 46; cf. DeMoss, *Holiness,* 121.

10. See, for example, Psalm 119:9-11; Ephesians 6:10-20; Hebrews 4:12.

11. Carlyle B. Haynes, *God Sent A Man* (Hagerstown, MD: Review and Herald, 1962), pp. 24-25.

PART II
HEALING THE PAINFUL WOUNDS
(What To Do When We Realize Our Choices Are Wrong)

“May I provide a simple formula by which you can measure the choices which confront you. It’s easy to remember: ‘You can’t be right by doing wrong; you can’t be wrong by doing right.’ Your personal conscience always warns you as a friend before it punishes you as a judge.”

—*Thomas S. Monson*

“Today I have given you the choice between life and death, between blessings and curses. . . . Oh, that you would choose life, so that you and your descendants might live!” (Deuteronomy 30:19, New Living Translation).

“The greatest power that a person possesses is the power to choose.”

—*J. Martin Kohe*

Chapter 5
The Balm for Our Wounds

Every wrong choice we make inflicts some wounds upon us—and even upon others. Depending on the nature of the wound, if they are not treated right away, complications and infections can set in, causing the wounds to become bigger, deeper, or more painful. In some cases, the wounds can be fatal.

The speedy healing of any wound involves three essential processes: careful examination, cleaning, and closing of the wound. Also, for healing to be effective and complete, the wounded must be willing to follow all the prescriptions and directives from the physician—even when the patient doesn't feel like doing so.

As in literal wounds, so are our spiritual wounds of sin—the consequences resulting from wrong choices. To experience healing from our wounds, we must go to the Great Physician and follow the course of treatment He has prescribed.

Forgiveness is the balm that Heaven has prescribed for our wounds of sin.[1] Unlike earthly physicians who consider some wounds as incurable, according to the Heavenly Physician, there is no wound of sin that cannot be healed. No matter how deep the wounds may be, no matter how sinful we may be, we all can be healed—that is, provided we follow the conditions set forth in God's Word. Only those who refuse God's healing balm and directives are incurable. When that happens the Great Physician abandons such people to their fate—death or judgment.[2]

The question before us is: How does a wounded person receive spiritual healing of forgiveness? What should we do when we realize the painful consequences of our choices?

This second section of *Healed Wounds, But Ugly Scars*—"Healing the Painful Wounds"—offers some biblical directions. It will affirm the availability of God's forgiveness to all and will explain how a sinner can put his or her life back together again.

In this particular chapter, I will draw from my earlier work—*Not for Sale*—to show that there is pardon even for those who have made the worst choices in life and who may even have committed the most egregious crimes.[3] In the subsequent chapters of Part II (i.e., chapters 6-10 of this book), I will draw upon a best-selling Christian classic to show how one can make the necessary U-turn and get back on track again.

Forgiveness: A Healing Balm for All

Is there hope for people who have knowingly and even ignorantly committed the most awful sins?

Yes, indeed, God *can* and *will* forgive. His forgiveness is the balm for our wounds. And Christ's dying prayer on Calvary's cross is the greatest evidence that forgiveness is available to all. His prayer, "Father, forgive them, for they don't know what they are doing" (Luke 23:32), is proof that not only will God forgive the actions of all those involved in the death of Christ—but also every sinner who is willing to accept His offer of forgiveness.

On Calvary's cross, Jesus didn't condemn those responsible for His death. He didn't utter any curses or attack His attackers. Though suffering injustice, though He didn't deserve what evil men were doing to Him, Christ did not blame anyone—though many were to blame. Instead, He said, *"Father forgive them, for they know not what they do"*!

No one standing near the cross expected Christ to offer forgiveness to those who were hurting Him. Yet He did. The amazing thing at Calvary was that while our Lord Jesus was being crucified, He "kept praying" that His murderers would be forgiven! The only words that kept coming from His lips were words of forgiveness, even explaining the reason for the action of His murderers: "For they do not know what they are doing"!

It is simply amazing: Calvary, the place where human beings did their worst, was also where God did His best. On the cross, God displayed His love for those who showed their hatred and contempt. Calvary is the place where Christ stretched out His arms, beckoning all humanity to come unto Him. For in His most agonizing moment,

Christ prays for His killers: "Father, forgive them, for they don't know what they are doing."

Christ's offer of forgiveness to those murdering Him was an incredible act. But the act also raises two profound questions: 1) Why forgive a person for what he does not know he is doing? And 2) Who are the "they" for whom Christ prayed?

1. The Guilt of Ignorance

The first question arising from Christ's dying prayer—namely, "Why forgive a person for what he does not know he is doing?"—raises the issue of the "guilt of ignorance." Can a person be held accountable for an offence of which he or she is not aware?

Notice that Jesus did not say that all sins done in ignorance lose, on that ground, their sinful character. Although the people "did not know what they were doing," they needed forgiveness, and Christ offered it. This fact reveals that ignorance does not absolve one of moral blame.

Forgiveness is only needed for the guilty. Nobody can forgive an innocent person. So when Jesus said, "Father, forgive them," He meant they were guilty. Then when He said, "For they don't know what they are doing," at the very least He meant, "they should have known what they were doing. And they are guilty for not knowing what they are doing." That is why they needed to be forgiven.

In other words, "I did not know" is not an excuse to absolve us from wrong-doing. Ignorance and guilt are not mutually exclusive. A person may do wrong ignorantly, yet be blameworthy and, therefore, need forgiveness.

The Bible teaches such a thing as "sinning through ignorance." Though this particular sin may differ in degree from willful, premeditated sin (and hence punishment or moral responsibility may differ on that account), it is sin, nonetheless.[4] Our Lord Himself confirms this teaching of "sinning through ignorance" when He teaches that "he who did not know, yet committed things deserving of stripes, shall be beaten with few" (Luke 12:48).

But it should also be observed that Christ's prayer on the cross not only declares our guilt—even the guilt resulting from our sins of ignorance—but also offers forgiveness at the same time. His prayer declares that we are guilty, *and* He simultaneously offers forgiveness. Not only did He say, "for they don't know what they are doing," but He also says, "Father, forgive them."

2. Extent of God's Forgiveness

The second question raised by Christ's prayer at Calvary is this: Who was He talking about when He said, "For *they* know not what they are doing?" Who are the "they" He was talking about, and who are the "them" for whom He was requesting forgiveness? These questions have to do with the extent of God's forgiveness.

The immediate context of Christ's prayer suggests that He was referring to the *Roman* soldiers. They were the ones carrying out the execution. They were the ones who were doing the dirty deed. They were the ones nailing Him to the cross. No doubt they had watched the proceedings of the trial and had seen Christ's demeanor all through the process. Like one of the soldiers at the cross who "glorified God, saying, 'Certainly this was a righteous Man!'" (Luke 23:47), the soldiers who nailed Christ to the cross could have known that He was innocent. Yet, they killed Him, perhaps on the lame excuse that they were just following orders. They were guilty.

But, the "they" in Christ's prayer also included the whole *Roman government, with Pontius Pilate* as its representative. Pilate could have changed the outcome. He could have followed his own gut conviction, if not the Roman law. He didn't have to cave in to the pressure of the crowd and the lure of his own ambition. He could have done something, but he didn't. Even when his own wife, who was warned in a dream, urged him to set Christ free, he didn't. He was guilty.

Included in the "they" are also *the religious authorities* and *the crowd at the trial.* They were the ones who, preferring Barabbas over Christ, handed Jesus over to Pilate. They knew, or should have known (like Nicodemus, the ruler of the synagogue) that Jesus was the Messiah. But when given the opportunity by Pilate to set Jesus free, they cried out, "Crucify Him!" They also were guilty.

And yes, the "they" also included *Judas*—the disciple who sold Jesus to the religious rulers. He had listened long to Christ's teachings and Jesus had pled with him personally.[5] Yet he joined in the plot to kill his Master.

But there is more to the "they." When Christ asked His Father for forgiveness, saying, "they don't know what they are doing," the "they" also included Christ's *own followers—the disciples who abandoned Him in the hour of His greatest need.* They probably could not have changed the course of events in opposition to the Roman army, the government authority, and the religious leaders. But they could have done something. They could have stood by Him, stayed with Him, been loyal to Him, and showed Him they cared. But they were afraid. They hid themselves away. They closed themselves in, cowering behind locked doors.

Above all, "they" is a reference to *all of us.* As we have shown in the previous section, both *Jews and Gentiles* are complicit in the shameful death of Christ. This includes *you and me*—those of us who daily crucify Christ afresh by our sins. Like all the others we also are guilty, even if we are ignorant. For we should have known better—at least we could have known.

Yes, we can identify some of the guilty ones by name: Judas, Annas, Caiaphas, Herod, Pilate, and Peter. In addition, the Roman soldiers were also guilty, and so were the other Jewish leaders such as the Pharisees and the scribes who conspired to put Him to death. The unnamed individuals in the crowd at the trial were also guilty. The spectators who were at Calvary to cheer, laugh, and mock were guilty. The entire nation of Israel and all Gentiles were guilty. And yes, we also are guilty. We are included among the "they."

Although guilty, Christ prayed for us all, saying, "Father, forgive them, for *they* don't know what they are doing."

The significance of Christ's dying prayer at Calvary is made more explicit in a prophecy recorded in Isaiah 53. In this Messianic prophecy, the prophet Isaiah explains that Christ's prayer was not just for them—the people who were immediately responsible for His death—but for all of us: "Because He poured out His soul unto death, and He was numbered with the transgressors, and *He bore the sin of many, and made intercession for the transgressors*" (Isaiah 53:12).

At Calvary, Christ "bore the sin of many, and made intercession for the transgressors." When the Bible says Christ bore the sins of "many," it means *all* sinners who accept His offer of salvation by believing in Him.[6] He made "intercession" for all sinners—that is, He prayed for all of us. This is the glory of the Christian gospel.

The Glory of the Gospel

Christ's prayer at the cross is the heart and glory of the Christian gospel—namely, that forgiveness is available to all who are willing to accept it. On Calvary's cross full atonement was made for the guilt of all sinners: covetous, envious, proud, liars, drunkards, prostitutes, adulterers, sexually immoral, racists, robbers, rebellious, murderers, etc. There is mercy for all who are willing to accept it.

In anticipation of this marvelous event at Calvary, the Old Testament prophets declared, "'Come now, let us reason together,' says the Lord. 'Though your sins are like scarlet, they shall be as white as snow; though they are red as crimson, they shall be like wool'" (Isaiah 1:18). Scarlet sins will be made as white as snow!

In a sense, the Bible can be read as a record of how God forgives sinners and transforms them into saints. We can trace back through the ages to find examples of God's loving forgiveness:

- King David's sins of adultery, dishonesty, and murder
- The many sins of the woman of Luke 7
- The prodigal son's riotous living in a distant city
- Simon Peter's triple denial of Christ by swearing and profanity
- Zacchaeus, a public robber
- Mary Magdalene, a common harlot
- Saul of Tarsus's merciless persecution of Christians
- The Corinthian church member who slept with his father's wife

Though sin is offensive to God, and though unconfessed sin can cost us our salvation, if we acknowledge our wrong-doing and change our ways, God will forgive us. The experience of the believers in the church of Corinth can be ours too:

> Do you not know that the unrighteous will not inherit the kingdom of God? Do not be deceived. Neither fornicators, nor idolaters, nor adulterers, nor homosexuals, nor sodomites, nor thieves, nor covetous, nor drunkards, nor revilers, nor extortioners will inherit the kingdom of God. *And such were some of you. But you were washed, but you were sanctified, but you were justified in the name of the Lord Jesus and by the Spirit of our God"* (1 Corinthians 6:9-11, emphasis supplied).[7]

God's forgiveness knows no bounds. Writes the Psalmist: "If You, Lord, should mark iniquities, O Lord, who could stand? But there is forgiveness with You, that You may be feared" (Psalm 130:3, 4). Although God will punish unrepentant evil-doers, the Bible makes clear that He is "merciful and gracious, longsuffering, and abounding in goodness and truth, keeping mercy for thousands, forgiving *iniquity* and *transgression* and *sin*" (Exodus 34:6, 7).

Each of these three words has a different connotation. *Iniquity* has to do with moral evil. *Transgression* signifies revolt or rebellion. *Sin* means an offence against the Most High God. These three terms cover every kind of evil possible. Whatever category of sin, God forgives it all. And His forgiveness is the healing balm for all our wounds.

The theme of divine forgiveness is at the very heart of the good news about Jesus Christ. When we acknowledge our sins, confess them, and make a commitment to turn away from them, Christ is always anxious to forgive us. The Psalmist says: "For You, Lord, are good, and ready to forgive, and abundant in mercy to all those who call upon You" (Psalm 86:5).

Christ's dying prayer at Calvary assures us that the Lord will never cast away a truly repentant soul. The following promises of His willingness to forgive will dispel any lingering doubts:

- " 'Come now, and let us reason together,' says the Lord, 'Though your sins are like scarlet, they shall be as white as snow; though they are red like crimson, they shall be as wool' " (Isaiah 1:18).

- "For You have cast all my sins behind Your back" (Isaiah 38:17).

- "As far as the east is from the west, so far has He removed our transgressions from us" (Psalm 103:12).

- "Who is a God like You, pardoning iniquity and passing over the transgression of the remnant of His heritage? He does not retain His anger forever, because He delights in mercy" (Micah 7:18).

- "Let the wicked forsake his way, and the unrighteous man his thoughts; let him return to the Lord, and He will have mercy on him; and to our God, for He will abundantly pardon" (Isaiah 55:7).

That God will forgive is further evidenced by the fact that among the 3,000 who repented and were baptized on the day of Pentecost were some of the people who had earlier on shouted, "Crucify Him" (Acts 2:36-41).

No sin is so dark that God won't forgive. We cannot out-sin the forgiveness of God if we truly repent, confess, and ask for forgiveness: "If we confess our sins, He is faithful and just to forgive us our sins and to cleanse us from all unrighteousness" (1 John 1:9).

There is a healing balm for all our wounds. If we repent—if we turn from our wrong-doing—God will *forgive* us and *cleanse* us from *all* unrighteousness. The message from Calvary's cross is that forgiveness is freely available to all who believe.

There's only one situation in which finding forgiveness is difficult. If we choose to remain in denial, if we remain unrepentant, Heaven cannot forgive us. That is, if we don't desire forgiveness, if we don't ask for it, or if we persistently refuse to respond to the invitation to repent, it is impossible to receive His forgiveness.

But when we acknowledge and repent of our sin, the Lord will not only forgive us, He will totally cleanse us of all our wrong-doing. In the next chapters, I'll refer to the Christian classic *Steps to Christ* to explain how this is possible—the steps necessary to experience complete healing from our wounds of sin.

Endnote

1. Jeremiah 8:22; Psalm 103:2-4; cf. Isaiah 30:26.

2. See, for example, Isaiah 1; Jeremiah 15:18; 30:11-13; Micah 1:9; Nahum 3:19.

3. Samuel Koranteng-Pipim, *Not for Sale: Integrity in a Culture of Silence* (Ann Arbor, MI: Berean Books, 2008), pp. 93-103.

4. This fact is also plainly taught in the Old Testament: "If a person sins, and commits any of these things which are forbidden to be done by the commandments of the Lord, though he does not know it, yet he is guilty and shall bear his iniquity. And he shall bring to the priest a ram without blemish from the flock, with your valuation, as a trespass offering. So the priest shall make atonement for him regarding his ignorance in which he erred and did not know it, and it shall be forgiven him" (Leviticus 5:17, 18). Thus, sins done in ignorance are still sin. Those who commit such sins need forgiveness, just as much as those who commit willful sins. In the New Testament we read that during the "times of ignorance God overlooked, but now commands all men everywhere to repent" (Acts 17:30). If one has to repent for things done in ignorance, the implication is that those acts are sin. Though one's punishment may be mitigated by certain factors, ignorance does not absolve one from the punishment one deserves. The apostle Paul judges his own past life on the same principle of "sinning through ignorance." When he persecuted the church, he did it ignorantly. He was honestly mistaken. He was "the least of the apostles," not worthy to be called an apostle because he persecuted the Church of God" (1 Corinthians 15:9).

5. See, for example, Matthew 26:17-25; John 12:1-7; 13:18-30.

6. That the "many" is a reference to all who believe is evident in a number of Bible passages. For example, referring to Christ's statement that He came in order to give "His life a *ransom for many*" (Matthew 20:28; Mark 10:45), the apostle Paul explains: "For there is one God, and one mediator between God and men, the man Christ Jesus; Who gave himself a *ransom for all,* to be testified in due time" (1 Timothy 2:5, 6). In other words, the "many" is not restrictive to a few people, but is to all, that is, to all who believe: "But *as many as received him,* to them gave he power to become the sons of God, even to them that believe on his name" (John 1:12). This message is also found in the favorite Bible passage, "For God so loved the world that He gave His only begotten Son, that *whoever believes in Him* should not perish but have everlasting life" (John 3:16).

7. The use of the past tense in 1 Corinthians 6:11 emphasizes that what the Corinthians were in the past is not what they are in the present, because they have been changed. The process by which this change takes place is defined by three terms: cleansing, sanctification, and justification. In the Greek, each verb is introduced by the strong adversative conjunction *alla,* a word normally translated in English as "but." Thus, the KJV states: "*but* ye are washed, *but* ye are sanctified, *but* ye are justified. . . ." The force of the word "but" (*alla*) is that it expresses a sharp contrast to what has come before. It also has a confirming or emphatic nuance. In other words, there was a radical difference between what the Corinthians were in the past and what they currently became when they were converted. The completeness of the forgiveness and transformation of the Corinthians can be ours today, when we acknowledge our wrong-doing and confess our sins.

Chapter 6
Examine the Wound

Our wrong choices have seriously wounded us. Forgiveness is the healing balm for the wounds of sin we have inflicted upon ourselves. The previous chapter of this book showed that, Jesus Christ, the Great Physician, is able and willing to heal all our wounds of sin—no matter how deep or sore they may be. Forgiveness is available to all who need it.

But exactly how do we go about experiencing this forgiveness? How can we experience freedom from sin's guilt? How can we be healed from our wounds?

This chapter—and the four chapters that follow it—provide a welcome help. They consist of selections from *Steps to Jesus*—a contemporary adaptation of the nineteenth-century devotional classic, *Steps to Christ.*[1]

This particular chapter explains that the first step to forgiveness is repentance—making a U-turn. To be healed from sin, we must not only admit that we are wounded; we must also be willing to examine the nature of the wound. Only then can we be free from our guilt.

Freedom from Guilt

How can a person be put right with God? How can a sinner be made righteous? Only through Christ can we find harmony with God and be made holy. But how are we to come to Christ?

Many people are asking this question. Crowds of people on the Day of Pentecost saw how sinful they were. They asked Peter and the other apostles, "What shall we do?" (Acts 2:37).

Peter said, "Each one of you must turn away from your sins," (verse 38). A few days later he answered the same question by saying, "Repent, then, and turn to God" (Acts 3:19).

To repent means to be sorry for sin and to turn away from it. We will not give up sin unless we see how sinful it is. There will be no real change in our lives until we stop loving sin and decide to turn from it.

False Repentance

Many people do not really understand true repentance. Millions are sorry that they have sinned. They even change their ways, because they are afraid that their wrongdoing will cause them suffering. But this is not true repentance; it is not the kind the Bible tells about. These people are sorry that sin may make them suffer, but they are not sorry for the sin itself.

Esau was sorry to lose forever his father's blessing and riches because of his sin. Balaam was afraid when he saw the angel standing in his pathway with a sword in his hand. He said, "I have sinned," because he was afraid of losing his life. But he was not really sorry for his sin. He did not change his mind or feel terrible about his evil plan.

Judas Iscariot sold his Lord to those who planned to kill Him. Then he cried out, "I have sinned by betraying an innocent man to death!" (Matthew 27:4). This confession was forced from his guilty heart by a terrible fear of punishment. He was afraid that he might have to suffer for what he had done, but he felt no deep, heart-breaking sorrow for selling the perfect Son of God to die. He was not sorry that he had turned away from Jesus, the Holy One of Israel.

When Pharaoh, king of Egypt, was being punished by God, he was willing to say he had sinned. He wanted to escape further pain and loss. But he turned against God again as soon as the suffering stopped.

All these men were sorry that sin had brought bad results, but they were not sorry for the sin itself.

True Repentance

When we yield to the influence of the Spirit of God, the conscience is awakened. We begin to see how broad and sacred is God's holy law, and that it is the basis of God's government in heaven and in earth. Jesus, "the light that comes into the world and shines on all people" (John 1:9), shines into the secret places of our mind and shows up the hidden thoughts. We see how righteous God is, and we feel afraid to come, guilty and unclean, before the Searcher of hearts. Then we see the love of God, the beauty of His holiness, and the joy of His purity. We desire to be made pure so that we can be friends with God again.

David's prayer after he had greatly sinned shows us what true sorrow is like. His repentance was sincere and deep. He did not try to make his wrong act seem small. He did not try to escape the result of what he had done. David saw that his sin was great and that his heart was unclean. He hated his sin. He prayed not only for forgiveness but for a clean heart. He wanted the joy of holiness – to be brought back into harmony with God. He wrote: "Happy are those whose sins are forgiven, whose wrongs are pardoned. Happy is the one whom the Lord does not accuse of doing wrong and who is free from deceit" (Psalm 32:1, 2).

"Be merciful to me, O God, because of your constant love. Because of your great mercy wipe away my sins! . . . I recognize my faults; I am always conscious of my sins. . . . Remove my sin, and I will be clean; wash me, and I will be whiter than snow. . . . Create a pure heart in me, O God, and put a new and loyal spirit in me. . . . Give me again the joy that comes from your salvation, and make me willing to obey you. . . . Spare my life, O God, and save me, and I will gladly proclaim your righteousness" (Psalm 51:1-14).

Repentance of this kind is beyond the reach of our own power. It comes only from Christ, who went to heaven and has given us spiritual gifts.

Common Mistakes

Many people do not understand repentance, so they fail to receive the help Christ wants to give them. They think they cannot come to Christ unless they first repent. They believe that repentance prepares the way for the forgiveness of their sins.

It is true that a person must repent before he is forgiven, for only when one is truly sorry for his sin will he feel the need of a Saviour. But must the sinner wait until he has repented before he can come to Jesus? Must the need for repentance keep the sinner away from the Saviour?

The Bible does not teach that the sinner must repent before he can accept Christ's invitation, "Come to me, all of you who are tired from carrying heavy loads, and I will give you rest" (Matthew 11:28). Christ's grace, His power, leads a person to truly repent. Peter made this clear when he said of Jesus, "Him hath God exalted with his right hand to be a Prince and a Saviour, for to give repentance to Israel, and forgiveness of sins" (Acts 5:31, KJV). The Spirit of Christ leads us to repent and be pardoned by God.

Every right desire comes from Christ. He is the only one who can make us hate sin. Every time we feel a desire for truth and purity, every time we see our own sinfulness, we can know that the Holy Spirit is working on our hearts.

Jesus said, "When I am lifted up from the earth, I will draw everyone to me" (John 12:32). Christ must be shown to the sinner as the Saviour who died for the sins of the world; and as we see the Son of God on the cross of Calvary we begin to understand God's plan to save us. Then the goodness of God leads us to repentance. When Christ died for sinners, He showed a love too great for us to understand. But as we see this love, it touches our hearts and affects our minds, and we become sorry for our sin.

Sometimes sinners feel ashamed of their sinful ways and give up some of their bad habits. They do this even though they do not know that they are being drawn to Christ. But whenever they try to change their ways because they have a sincere desire to do right, it is Christ's power that is moving them. His Spirit is influencing their minds and helping them to live better lives.

As Christ draws sinners to look at His cross and see that their sins caused Him to die, their consciences are troubled. Then they see how terrible their sins are. They begin to understand something of the righteousness of Christ. They cry out, "What is sin? Why did Christ have to die? Was all this love and suffering demanded to save our lives? Did He suffer all this so that we could have everlasting life?"

The sinner may resist God's love and refuse to be drawn to Christ, but if he does not resist, he will be drawn to Him. He will learn about God's plan to save sinners. He will come to the cross and repent of the sins that caused the sufferings of God's dear Son.

The same God who controls nature speaks to the hearts of people. He gives them a great desire for something they do not have. The things of the world cannot satisfy this desire. God is telling people to find the grace of Christ and the joy of holiness. These alone can bring peace and rest.

Our Saviour is trying all the time to draw people's minds away from the worldly pleasures to the wonderful blessings that Christ can give. To these people who are trying to find water in the dry wells of the world, He says, "Come, whoever is thirsty; accept the water of life as a gift, whoever wants it" (Revelation 22:17).

If you have a desire for something better than the world can give, this is God speaking to you. Ask Him to give you repentance and show you Christ in His infinite love and perfect purity.

The Saviour's life makes plain that the law of God is based on love to God and other people. To be unselfish, loving, and kind was what Jesus lived for. So, as we look at our Saviour and light from Him falls on us, we see how sinful we really are.

Correct Perception

We may feel, as Nicodemus did, that our lives are good and that we do not need to humble ourselves before God like a common sinner. But when the light from Christ shines into our hearts, we see that we are not pure. We see that we are enemies of God and that every act of life is selfish. When we see His righteousness, we shall know that "even our best actions are filthy through and through" (Isaiah 64:6). Only Christ's sacrifice can take away our sins and make us clean. Only Christ can change our lives until we are like Him.

One ray of light from God's glory shows every spot and weakness in our character. One brief view of the purity of Christ makes our lives look unclean. It shows plainly that we have evil desires, unfaithful hearts, and impure speech. We see that we are not obeying God's law. As the Spirit of God searches our hearts, we feel unhappy about ourselves. We look at Christ's spotless character and hate our evil ways.

The prophet Daniel was visited by an angel from heaven. Glory shone all around the angel, and Daniel was overcome as he thought of his own weakness and lack of perfection. He wrote, "I had no strength left, and my face was so changed that no one could have recognized me" (Daniel 10:8).

Any person who sees this glory from heaven will hate his own selfishness and self-love. He will search for purity of heart through Christ's righteousness. He will want to keep God's law and have a Christlike character.

Paul wrote of his own righteousness: "As far as a person can be righteous by obeying the commandments of the Law, I was without fault" (Philippians 3:6). When he noted just the words of the law, then looked at his life, he could see no fault in himself. But when he looked at the deep meaning of the law, he saw himself as God saw him. He bowed down and confessed his guilt.

Paul wrote, "That is why I felt fine so long as I did not understand what the law really demanded. But when I learned the truth, I realized that I had broken the law and was a sinner, doomed to die" (Romans 7:9, TLB). When Paul saw how holy the law was, sin looked terrible. He no longer felt proud, but humble.

God does not look at all sins as equally bad. To Him, as to us, some sins are worse than others. But even if some wrong acts appear small to us, no sin seems small to God. Human judgment is often wrong, but God sees things as they really are. People dislike a drunk person and say his sin will keep him out of heaven. But often these same people say nothing against pride, selfishness, and greed. Yet these are sins that especially offend God because they are so different from His loving character. Unselfish love fills every heart in heaven.

A person who makes a big mistake and sins may feel ashamed. He may feel that he needs the grace of God. But a proud person feels no need, so he closes his heart against Christ and the wonderful blessings He came to give.

Jesus once told a story about a tax collector who bowed his head and said, "God, have pity on me, a sinner" (Luke 18:13). He thought of himself as a wicked man, and other people looked upon him in the same way. But he felt his need of a Saviour and came to God with his load of sin and shame. He asked for God's mercy. His heart was open for the Spirit of God to come in and set him free from the power of sin.

Then Jesus told about a Pharisee who thanked God that he was not like other men. The Pharisee's prayer showed that his heart was closed against the Spirit of God. Because he was a long way from God, he did not see how sinful he was. He did not compare his life with God's holiness. He felt no need, and he received nothing.

If we see that we are sinful, we must not wait to make ourselves better. We must not think that we are not good enough to come to Christ. Can we expect to become better by just trying, in our own strength? "Can people change the color of their skin, or a leopard remove his spots? If they could, then you that do nothing but evil could learn to do what is right" (Jeremiah 13:23).

God is the only one who can help us. We must not wait for someone to beg us to change or for a better chance or until we gain control of a bad temper. We can do nothing of ourselves. We must come to Christ just as we are.

Our heavenly Father is a God of love and mercy. But we must not think He will save us if we turn from His grace. The cross of Jesus shows how terrible sin is. When people say that God is so kind He will not cast off the sinner, they should look at the cross. Only through Christ's sacrifice can we be saved. Without this sacrifice we could not escape from the power of sin. Without it, we could not share heaven with the angels. Without it, we could not have spiritual life.

To save us, Christ took our guilt on Himself and suffered in our place. The love, suffering, and death of the Son of God show us how terrible sin is. They also tell us that the only way to escape from sin is to come to Christ. Our only hope for a life in heaven is to give ourselves to the Saviour.

Timely Cautions

Sinners sometimes excuse themselves by saying of people who claim to be Christians, "I am as good as they are. They do not act any better than I do. They love pleasure as much as I do. They love to please themselves."

In this way sinners make the faults of others an excuse for not doing their own duty. But the sins and weaknesses of others do not excuse anyone, for the Lord has not asked us to take sinful people as a pattern. The spotless Son of God has been given as our example. Those who complain about the wrongdoing of others should themselves show a better way of living. If they know how a Christian should act, is not their sin much greater? They know what is right, yet they refuse to do it.

We must not delay turning from sin and coming to Jesus. We must seek for a pure heart through Him. Thousands and thousands of people have made the mistake of waiting, and it has cost them eternal life.

Life on earth is short and not at all certain. We do not think often enough about the terrible danger of delaying to yield to the voice of God's Holy Spirit. Delaying to obey God is really choosing to live in sin. And even small sins are dangerous. The sins that we do not overcome will overcome us and destroy us.

Adam and Eve let themselves believe that eating the forbidden fruit was so small a matter that it could not cause the terrible results that God had said would come. But this "small" matter was disobeying God's unchangeable, holy law. Disobedience separated the human family from God and let sorrow and death come into the world. Century after century a never-ending sad cry has gone up from the earth. The whole world is suffering because man disobeyed God. Heaven itself has felt the effects. Christ had to die on Calvary because man broke the divine law. Let us never think of sin as a small thing.

Every sin, every turning away from the grace of God, hardens our hearts. It leads us to make wrong choices. It keeps us from understanding God's love. Sin makes us less willing to obey, less able to yield to God's Holy Spirit.

Many people know they are doing wrong, but they do not change their ways. They believe they can change whenever they choose. They think they can turn from God again and again and still hear His call of mercy. They follow Satan, but they plan to turn quickly to God if something terrible happens to them. But this is not easy to do. Sin changes a person's desires and habits. After sin has molded the character, few people want to be like Jesus.

Even one wrong thing in the character or one sinful desire that we will not give up will finally stop the gospel's power from changing us. Every time we give in to Satan, we turn more from God. A person who finally will not listen to or obey God's word is but reaping the result of his own choices. In the Bible we read Solomon's most wise but terrible warning about playing around with evil. He wrote, "The sins of the wicked are a trap. They get caught in the net of their own sin" (Proverbs 5:22).

Christ is ready to set us free from sin, but He does not force us to stop sinning and choose His way. If we do not desire to be free, if we will not accept His grace, what more can He do? We will destroy ourselves by turning away from His love. Paul wrote, "Listen! This is the hour to receive God's favor. Today is the day to be saved!" "If you hear God's voice today, do not be stubborn" (2 Corinthians 6:2; Hebrews 3:7,8).

Go To Him Now

God said that people "look on the outward appearance, but I look at the heart" (1 Samuel 16:7). In our hearts, with all their joys and sorrows, is much that is impure and dishonest. But God knows our desires. He knows what we want to do. We must go to Him, all stained with sin, and open ourselves to His all-seeing eyes. We should say as David did, "Examine me, O God, and know my mind; test me, and discover my thoughts. Find out if there is any evil in me and guide in me in the everlasting way" (Psalm 139:23, 24).

Many of us accept God with our minds, but our hearts are not changed. We should pray, "Create a pure heart in me, O God, and put a new and loyal spirit in me" (Psalm 51:10). We must be honest with ourselves. We must be as sincere in this as if our very lives were in danger. It is a matter to be settled between us and God-and settled forever. Hope without action will not save us.

We should study God's Word and pray. His Word teaches us about the law of God. It tells us about the life of Christ and how to be holy. "Try to live a holy life, because no one will see the Lord without it" (Hebrews 12:14). God's word makes us feel how terrible sin is, and it shows us how to be saved. We must listen to it and obey it, for it is God speaking to us.

As we see how terrible sin is we see ourselves as we really are. But we must not lose hope and become discouraged. Christ came to save sinners.

We do not need to try to get God to be our friend and love us. He already loves us and is "making all human beings his friends through Christ" (2 Corinthians 5:19).

God is drawing the hearts of His sinful children to Himself with His gentle love. He is much more patient with our faults and mistakes than are our earthly parents. He wants to save all His children. He gently and kindly invites the sinner to come to Him and the wanderer to return. All God's promises, all His warnings, tell us of His eternal love.

At times, Satan comes to us to tell us that we are great sinners. But when he comes, we must look to our Redeemer and talk of His power and goodness. As we look to Him, He will help us. We will tell Satan that we know we have sinned, but "Christ Jesus came into the world to save sinners" (1 Timothy 1:15). We may be saved by His perfect love.

Jesus asked Simon about two people who owed money. One owed his master a small sum of money; the other owed a very large sum. The master forgave them both. Christ asked Simon which man would love his master most. Simon said, "I supposed … that it would be the one who was forgiven most" (Luke 7:43).

We have been great sinners, but Christ died so that we could be forgiven. His priceless sacrifice is worth enough to pay for our sins. Those who are forgiven most will love Him most. They will be closest to Him in heaven, and they will praise Him for His great love and infinite sacrifice.

When we fully understand the love of God, we most clearly see how terrible sin is. When we see how far He has reached down to touch us and save us, our hearts are made tender. When we understand something of Christ's sacrifice, then we are truly sorry for our sins, and our hearts are full of love for Him.

Endnotes

1. The author of *Steps to Christ,* Ellen G. White (1827-1915), was a woman of remarkable spiritual gifts who lived most of her life during the nineteenth century, yet through her writings and public ministry she has made a revolutionary impact on millions of people around the world. She was a contemporary of Christian giants like Dwight L. Moody (1837-1899), F. B. Meyer (1847-1929), Henry Drummond (1851-1897), R. A.

Torrey (1856-1928), and Ralph Connor (1860-1937). During Ellen G. White's lifetime, she wrote more than 5,000 periodical articles and 49 books. Today, including compilations from her manuscripts, more than 100 titles are available in English. She is the most translated woman writer in the entire history of literature and the most translated American author of either gender, measured by the number of languages having at least one of her works. Her literary productions deal with a wide range of subjects—spirituality, theology, education, health, family, etc. But she was more than a prolific author. While the world is only now coming to appreciate her deep spiritual and practical insights, millions have always recognized her as a recipient of the true gift of prophecy. Her life-changing masterpiece on successful Christian living, *Steps to Christ* has been published in about 150 languages, with well over tens of millions copies in circulation. The book deals with the central issue of how to become and remain a Christian—the concern at the core of Mrs. White's voluminous writing. Mrs. White's crowning literary achievement is the five-volume "Conflict of the Ages" series, which traces the conflict between good and evil from its origin to its dramatic, soon-to-unfold conclusion. It is widely acclaimed as the best devotional commentary on the entire Bible. Ellen G. White came from a Methodist background and became one of the pioneers of the Seventh-day Adventist Church, one of the fastest growing Protestant denominations in the world. In this chapter and the subsequent chapters of Part II (i.e., in chapters 6-10 of this book), I will reproduce the text from her book *Steps to Jesus,* a contemporary adaptation of *Steps to Christ* (1892). The selections from *Steps to Jesus* [Hagerstown, Maryland: Review and Herald, 1997), pp. 18-64, are used with the permission of the Ellen G. White Estates, owner of the copyright of the book. I have inserted subheadings in the text of *Steps to Jesus* to allow for easier reading. Observe that while E. G. White's thoughts have been retained in *Steps to Jesus,* hard-to-understand phrases in *Steps to Christ* have been restated in everyday language, the vocabulary has been simplified, and long sentences have been shortened. These changes have been made according to carefully established guidelines. With only a few exceptions, Scripture passages from Today's English Version have been substituted for the King James Version of the Bible. Note also that the main headings for the E. G. White selections in chapters 6-10 of this book—"Freedom from Guilt," "A Clear Conscience," "Total Commitment," "Discovering Peace of Mind," and "Becoming a New Person"—come from *Peace Above the Storm: Freedom from Worry, Guilt and Fear* (Nampa, Idaho: Pacific Press, 1994).

Chapter 7
Cleansing the Wound

Cleansing (or cleaning) is one of the three essential processes necessary for the speedy healing of any bodily wound. (The other two are careful examination and closing). Cleansing can be accomplished using a number of different liquid solutions, including tap water, sterile normal saline, or an antiseptic solution.

If there has been some bleeding, cleansing enables those affected by injury to come to terms with the true nature of their wounds. More importantly, cleansing prevents infection, by keeping the wounds free from dirt, impurities, germs, and other foreign matter.

Cleansing is a fitting analogy for the preparation needed to receive complete forgiveness, the true healing for our wounds of sin.

How do we "come clean" with our spiritual wounds? How do we experience clean consciences after we recognize our sins? And what are the specific conditions necessary in order to make things right with God and with those who suffer from the consequences of our choices and actions?

This chapter—which could very well be titled "Experiencing A Clear Conscience"—will address the above questions.[1]

A Clear Conscience

You will never succeed in life if you try to hide your sins. Confess them and give them up; then God will show mercy to you" (Proverbs 28:13).

The rules for receiving the mercy of God are simple, fair and reasonable. The Lord does not ask us to do something hard and painful so that our sins may be forgiven. We do not need to make long, tiring journeys. We cannot pay for our sins by suffering. Anyone who confesses his sins and turns away from them will receive mercy.

The apostle James says, "Confess your faults one to another, and pray for one another, that ye may be healed" (James 5:15, KJV). We confess our sins to God, for only He can forgive them. We confess our faults to one another. If we have offended a friend or neighbor, we must admit the wrong, and it is his duty to forgive freely. Then we are to ask God to forgive us, because the neighbour belongs to God. When we hurt him, we sin against the Creator and redeemer.

We take the case to Jesus Christ , our great High Priest. "Our High Priest is not one who can not feel sympathy for our weaknesses....We have a High Priest who was tempted in every way that we are, but did not sin" (Hebrews 4:15). He is able to wash away every spot of sin.

Be Humble

We must humble ourselves before God and admit that we have sinned. This is the first rule for being accepted by God. If we have not repented and humbled ourselves, confessing our sins, we have not truly asked for forgiveness. If we do not hate our sins, we do not want truly to be forgiven, and we do not find the peace of God.

If we have not been forgiven of our sins, the only reason is that we are not willing to humble ourselves. We are not willing to follow the rules set forth in the Bible. God has carefully told us what we are to do. We must open our hearts and freely admit we have sinned. We should not do this in a light or careless way. Nor should we be forced to do it. We must realize how bad sin is and hate it.

If we truly confess, pouring out our hearts to God, He will hear and pity us. The psalmist, David, wrote, "The Lord is nigh unto them that are of a broken heart; and saveth such as be of a contrite spirit" (Psalm 34:18, KJV).

Be Specific

True confession names the sin. It tells exactly what was done. A person may need to confess some sins only to God. Or he may need to go to some person and tell him that he is sorry he has hurt him. He may need to confess some sins in public. But every time a person confesses, he should name the sin of which he is guilty.

In the days of Samuel the people of Israel were not following God. They had lost faith in God and felt He was no longer able to lead them. They did not feel God's power, nor did they trust Him to care for them.

They turned away from the great Ruler of the universe and asked for a king such as other nations had.

God gave His people a king, but they had many troubles. Before they could find peace with God they made this confession: "Now we realize that, besides all our sins, we have sinned by asking for a king" (1 Samuel 12:19). They had to confess the exact sin that had caused their trouble. They had not been thankful to God for His leading, and this had cut them off from Him.

Sincere Repentance and Reformation

God can not accept our confession unless we repent and give up our sins. We must make decided changes in our lives. When we are truly sorry for sin, we will give up everything that is not pleasing to God. The work that we must do is plainly set before us: "Wash yourselves clean. Stop all this evil that I see you doing. Yes, stop doing evil and learn to do right. See that justice is done—help those who are oppressed, give orphans their rights, and defend widows" (Isaiah 1:16, 17). "If he [an evil man] returns the security he took for a loan or gives back what he stole—if he stops sinning and follows the laws that give life, he will not die, but live" (Ezekiel 33:15).

Paul says that changes take place when a person repents: "See what God did with this sadness of yours: how earnest it has made you, how eager to prove your innocence! Such indignation, such alarm, such feelings, such devotion, such readiness to punish wrong doing! You have shown yourselves to be without fault in the whole matter" (2 Corinthians 7:11).

No Excuses or Self-Justification

When sin dulls the moral senses, the sinner does not see what is wrong with his character. His sins do not look very bad to him. He is almost blind to them unless the power of the Holy Spirit opens his eyes. A person who is not led by the Holy Spirit is not sincere and in earnest when he confesses. He excuses his sins. He says he would not have done wrong if certain conditions had been different.

After Adam and Eve ate the forbidden fruit, they were ashamed and afraid. At first their only thought was how to excuse their sin and escape death. When the Lord asked about their sin, Adam blamed God and

Eve. He said, "The woman you put here with me gave me the fruit and I ate it." The woman blamed the snake. She said, "The snake tricked me into eating it" (Genesis 3:12, 13). She was saying to God, "Why did You make the snake? Why did You let him come into Eden?" She was excusing herself and blaming God for her sin.

The desire to make excuses for one's sins comes from Satan and is shared by all people. But confessing by blaming someone else is not God's way, and He will not accept it.

True repentance will lead a person to admit his guilt without trying to act innocent or making excuses. Like the tax collector of whom Jesus spoke, he will pray without even lifting his eyes to heaven, "God, have pity on me, a sinner." God will forgive those who admit they are guilty, for Jesus gave His life to save sinners who repent. He is the great High Priest in heaven.

We read in the Bible of people who truly repented. They were humble and confessed their sins. They did not try to make excuses or defend what they had done. The apostle Paul told of his sin of trying to kill the Christians. He did not try to make it appear small. He made it sound as bad as he could. He said: "I received authority from the chief priests and put many of God's people in prison; and when they were sentenced to death, I also voted against them. Many times I had them punished in the synagogues and tried to make them deny their faith. I was so furious with them that I even went to foreign cities to persecute them" (Acts 26:10, 11). Paul was eager to say, "Christ Jesus came into the world to save sinners. I am the worst of them" (1 Timothy 1:15).

A broken hearted person, humbled by true repentance, will see how much God loves him. He will understand the cost of Calvary. The sinner who is really sorry will confess. He will come to God as freely as a son comes to a loving father. John wrote, "If we confess our sins to God, he will keep his promise and do what is right: he will forgive us our sins and purify us from all wrongdoing" (1 John 1:9).

Endnote

1. "Experiencing A Clear Conscience" is chapter 4 of E. G. White's *Steps to Jesus,* where it is titled "Confession."

Chapter 8
Trust the Physician

In major surgical operations, patients literally trust their lives in the hands of the physician. They often sign documents, giving full permission to the surgeon to do whatever he deems is in the best interest of the patient.

In a similar way, a whole-hearted submission to Jesus Christ, the Master Physician, is crucial for the complete healing of our spiritual wounds. We must totally surrender or yield ourselves to His full control.

It is not possible for us, of ourselves, to heal our wounds of sin. All our attempts through education, good manners, willpower, and New Year resolutions, may help us in doing right things. But they cannot change our hearts and make our lives pure. Only the Master Physician can heal us from within. We must be willing to trust our lives completely into His hands for this supernatural operation called conversion.[1]

In this chapter of *Healed Wounds, But Ugly Scars,* we shall explain the nature of total surrender and how to do so. We shall discover that it all depends on the right use of the power of choice God has given us. Although we cannot change our own hearts, and although we cannot by ourselves give our love to God, we can *choose* to give our lives to Him. Saying "Yes" to Him every day, choosing His lordship, enables Him to come into our lives and change us completely.

Our presentation in this chapter focuses on the total committal or surrender of our lives to Christ. It is also found in *Steps to Jesus,* under the title "Consecration."[2]

Total Commitment

God's promise is "You will seek me, and you will find me because you will seek me with all your heart" (Jeremiah 29:13).

We must give all of our heart to God, or we cannot be changed to be like Him. Our sinful hearts are unlike God, and naturally turn from Him. The Bible describes the way we are: "spiritually dead"; "your heart and mind are sick"; "not a healthy spot on your body" (Ephesians 2:1; Isaiah 1:5, 6). Sinners are held fast by Satan. They are in "the trap of the Devil, who had caught them and made them obey his will" (2 Timothy 2:26).

God wants to heal us. He wants to set us free. To do this He must change us entirely so that we have new desires and habits. But He cannot do this until we give our selves completely to Him.

The Greatest Battle

The battle against self is the greatest battle ever fought. It is hard for us to give ourselves to God and let Him control our minds. But we must let God rule or He cannot make us new and holy.

Satan wants us to believe that we will be slaves in God's kingdom, blindly submitting to unreasonable demands. He says that God asks us to obey Him without giving reasons for his commands. But this is not true. We serve God with our reason as well as our conscience. God says to the people He has made, "Come now, and let us reason together" (Isaiah 1:18, KJV). God does not force us to obey. He cannot accept our worship unless we give it freely and with the mind.

Being forced to obey God would prevent us from developing our minds and characters. We would be like machines, and this is not what our Creator wants. He wants us, the crowning work of Creation, to make the best possible use of our minds and bodies. He teaches us about the great blessings He wants to bring us through His grace.

God invites us to give ourselves to Him so that He may guide us and carry out His plans for us. He gives us the right to choose what we shall do. We may choose to be set free from sin and share in the wonderful liberty that He gives His children.

Give Up All

When we give ourselves to God, we give up all that would separate us from Him. The Saviour said, "None of you can be my disciple unless you give up everything you have" (Luke 14:33). We must give up everything that takes our hearts away from God.

Many people worship riches. The desire for wealth and the love of money bind them to Satan. Others desire honor more than anything else. They want people to look up to them and praise them. Still others wish for an easy, selfish life with freedom from care. But we must turn away from all these. We cannot belong half to God and half to the world. We are God's children only when we are entirely His.

Some people say that they serve God, but they try to obey His law without His help. By their own works they try to develop a good character and receive salvation. Their hearts are not moved by the love of Christ. They try to do good works because they think God requires this in order for them to reach heaven. Such religion is worth nothing.

When Christ lives in us, we will be filled with His love. The joy of His friendship will make us want to be near Him. We shall think about Him so much that we will forget our selfish desires. Love for him will guide every action. If we feel the love of God, we will not ask how little we can do to obey Him. We will try to do all that our Redeemer wants. People who say they are Christians and not feel deep love for Christ are using words without meaning. To follow Christ is hard work for them.

Is It Too Much?

Should we feel it is too much to give all to Christ? We must ask ourselves the question, "What has Christ given for me?" The Son of God gave all—life and love and suffering—to save us. Can we, who are not worth this great love, keep back our hearts from Him?

Every moment of our lives we have received the blessings of His grace. Because of this we can never really know from how much trouble we have been saved. Can we look at the One who died for our sins and turn from such love? Our Lord of glory humbled Himself. Shall we complain because we must fight against selfishness and be humble?

Many proud hearts are asking, "Why do I need to humble myself and be sorry for my sins before I am sure that God will accept me?" I point you to Christ. He was sinless. He was the Prince of heaven, and yet He took our place and carried all our sins. "He willingly gave his life and shared the fate of evil men. He took the place of many sinners and prayed that they might be forgiven" (Isaiah 53:12).

What Do We Really Give Up?

What do we give when we give Him everything? We give Jesus a sinful heart for Him to make pure and clean. We ask Him to save us by His infinite love. And yet people think it is hard to give up all! I am ashamed to hear these words spoken; I am ashamed to write them.

God does not ask us to give up anything that is good for us to keep. He is thinking of what is best for us. I wish that all who have not chosen Christ could realize this. Christ has something far better for them than they could ask for themselves. People are not being fair to themselves when they go against what God wants.

We can find no real joy in walking in the path He tells us not to take. He knows what is good for us, and He has the best plan for each person. The path of disobeying God is the path of unhappiness and death.

Do not think that God likes to see His children suffer. All heaven is interested in our happiness. Our heavenly Father does not keep us from doing anything that will bring us true joy. He asks us to turn away form wrong habits and other things that will bring us suffering. He knows they will keep us from happiness and heaven.

The world's Redeemer accepts people as they are, with all their weaknesses and many faults. But He will wash away their sins and redeem through His blood. He will satisfy the desires of all who are willing to bear His load and share His work. He wants to give peace and rest to all who come to Him. He asks them to do only those things that will lead to great happiness. Those who do not obey cannot know this pleasure. True joy is to have Christ, the hope of glory, in the life.

How Do We Surrender to God?

Many people are asking, "*How* can I give myself to God?" They want to give themselves to Him, but their moral strength is weak. They doubt God and are controlled by sinful habits. Their promises are easily broken, like ropes of sand. They cannot control their thoughts or their desires. Because they cannot keep their promises, they lose confidence in themselves and wonder if they are sincere. They feel that God cannot accept them. But they must not lose hope.

We all need to understand the value of willpower. The power of choice is the ruling power in life. Everything depends on the right use of this power. God has given the power of choice to each person, and it is theirs to use. We cannot change our hearts. We cannot by ourselves give our love to God. But we can *choose* to serve Him. We can give Him the powers of our mind. Then He will help us choose the right way. Our whole being will be guided by the Spirit of Christ. We will love God, and our thoughts will be like His.

It is right that we should desire to be good and to be holy. But we must not stop there. These desires will not help us. Many people will be lost while hoping and desiring to be Christians. They do not come to the place where they yield the powers of the mind to God. They do not choose to be Christians.

An entire change may be made in our lives through the right use of the power of choice. When we put ourselves on God's side, He gives us His great power to hold us. By giving ourselves to God each day we will be able to live a new life, the life of faith.

Endnotes

1. Writes E. G. White: "It is impossible for us, of ourselves, to escape from the pit of sin in which we are sunken. Our hearts are evil, and we cannot change them. "Who can bring a clean thing out of an unclean? No one!." "The carnal mind is enmity against God; for it is not subject to the law of God, nor indeed can be." Job 14:4; Romans 8:7. Education, culture, the exercise of the will, human effort, all have their proper sphere, but here they are powerless. They may produce an outward correctness of behavior, but they cannot change the heart; they cannot purify the springs of life. There must be a power working from within, a new life from above, before men can be changed from sin to holiness. That power is Christ. His grace alone can quicken [give life to] the lifeless faculties of the soul, and attract it to God, to holiness." See, E. G. White, *Steps to Christ,* p. 18.

2. See chapter 5 of E. G. White's *Steps to Jesus,* pp. 37-45.

Chapter 9
Experiencing the Healing

Thus far, we have been discussing what to do when we realize our choices have inflicted serious wounds upon us. In the previous chapters of Part II of *Healed Wounds, But Ugly Scars,* we've talked about forgiveness as the healing balm we need for our sins. Experiencing forgiveness is to be whole again. The journey towards this total healing from our wounds of sin calls for repentance (freedom from guilt), confession (experiencing a clear conscience), and consecration (total commitment or surrender).

In this chapter, we shall add another vital component: The need for *ongoing* faith in Christ and complete acceptance of His Word. We experience the healing of forgiveness when we believe or trust in Him.

Trust is a defining element in any interpersonal relationship. It sustains the relationship and ensures peace of mind, especially during very difficult times in the relationship. But trust is particularly crucial to the patient-physician relationship. For a speedy and complete healing, patients must at all times know that their doctors seek their very best interests. Also, they must *always* have faith in the competence and wisdom of their physicians.

When patients have full confidence in their physicians, they wholeheartedly accept the doctors' diagnoses, prescriptions, and prognoses of their conditions—even when their doctors' opinions go against their feelings and inclinations. Absolute trust in the doctors' assurances gives peace of mind to the patients.

In much the same way, our journey towards complete healing from our wounds of sin requires an ongoing faith in Christ and complete acceptance of what the Master Physician says about our conditions. Absolute trust in His promises gives us the peace of mind we need to experience the fullness of healing.

Our spiritual healing can be impeded or hastened by the level of trust we repose in Christ. For example, there will be times when we shall doubt if, indeed, our sins have been truly forgiven and we are saved. There will also be moments when we shall be discouraged, feeling that no change is taking place in our conditions. During such periods, it is the assurances from God's Word that will sustain us in the healing process. God's promises provide us with the peace of mind we need.

This chapter will discuss how we can be certain that our sins have been forgiven. It will also reveal what we should do when there's a clash between how we really *feel* and what the Bible promises say. These issues are vital in how we experience complete healing from our wounds of sin. The discussion is found in chapter six of the devotional classic *Steps to Jesus,* where it appears under the title "Faith and Acceptance." I will employ the title "Discovering Peace of Mind."

Discovering Peace of Mind

As God's Holy Spirit brings to life the spiritual powers of your mind, you begin to see how evil and strong sin is. You feel the guilt and sorrow it brings, and you hate it. You feel that sin has separated you from God. Its power has made you a slave. The more you try to escape, the more you know that you cannot help yourself. You see that your life has been filled with selfishness and sin. Your heart is unclean and your desires are not pure. You want to be forgiven, to be clean, to be set free. But what can you do to be one with God and to be like Him?

You need peace – Heaven's forgiveness and peace and love. Money cannot buy that peace. Study will not give it. The mind cannot find it. Being wise will not provide it. You can never hope to receive this peace by your own work and power.

God offers His peace to you as a gift. 'It will cost you nothing!" (Isaiah 55:1). It is yours if you will reach out your hands and take it. The Lord says, "You are stained red with sin, but I will wash you as clean as snow. Although your stains are deep red, you will be as white as wool" (Isaiah 1:18). "I will give you a new heart and a new mind" (Ezekiel 36:26).

Fully Believe Him

You have confessed your sins and chosen to put them out of your life. You have decided to give yourself to God. Now go to Him and ask Him to wash away your sins. Ask Him to give you a new heart, a new mind. Then believe that He does this, *because He has promised.* Jesus taught this lesson when He was on the earth. You must believe that you receive the gift God promises and that it is yours.

Jesus healed the sick people who had faith in His power. Healing them made them able to see that He could help them in other ways. It led them to believe in His power to forgive sin. Jesus explained this when He was healing a man who was too sick to get out of his bed. He said, "I will prove to you, then, that the Son of Man has authority on earth to forgive sins." Jesus then spoke to the sick man, "Get up, pick up your bed, and go home!" (Matthew 9:6).

John, the disciple of Jesus, told us why Christ healed people. He wrote, "These have been written in order that you may believe that Jesus is the Messiah, the Son of God, and that through your faith in him you may have life" (John 20:31).

Read the Bible stories about Jesus healing the sick. From them you can learn something of how to believe in Him for the forgiveness of sins. Turn to the story of the sick man at the pool of Bethesda. The poor man was helpless. He had not walked for 38 years. Yet Jesus said to him, "Get up, pick up your bed, and go home!"

The sick man did not say, "Lord, if You make me well, I will obey Your word." No, he believed Christ's word. He believed he was made well, and that very moment he tried to walk. He chose to walk. And he did walk. He acted on the word of Christ, and God gave the power. The man was healed.

Now look at yourself. You are a sinner. You can do nothing to take away your past sins. You cannot change your heart or make yourself holy. But God promises to do all this for you through Christ. Believe that promise. Confess your sins and give yourself to God. Choose to serve Him. God will surely keep His promise to you if you do this. When you believe, God acts. You will be made clean and whole, just as Christ gave the sick man power to walk when he believed that he was healed. It is so if you believe it.

Not About Feelings

Do not wait to *feel* that you are made whole. Say, "I believe it. It is so, not because I feel it, but because God has promised."

Jesus said, "When you pray and ask for something, believe that you have received it, and you will be given whatever you ask for" (Mark 11:24). There is something important to remember in this promise. You must pray for those things that God wants you to have. God wants to free you from sin and make you His child. He wants to give you power to live a holy life.

You may pray for these blessings and believe that you receive them. Then you may thank God that you *have* received them. You may go to Jesus and be made clean and stand before God's law without shame or sadness. "There is no condemnation now for those who live in union with Christ Jesus" (Romans 8:1).

When you belong to Christ, you are not your own, for you are bought with a price. "God paid a ransom to save you..., and the ransom he paid was not mere gold or silver....But he paid for you with the priceless lifeblood of Christ, the sinless, spotless Lamb of God" (1 Peter 1:18, 19, TLB). Because you believe what God has said, the Holy Spirit creates a new life in your heart. You are as a child born into the family of God, and He loves you as He loves His own Son.

Now that you have given yourself to Jesus, do not turn back. Do not take yourself away from Him. Day after day say, "I am Christ's. I have given myself to Him." Ask Him to give you His Spirit and keep you by His grace. You became His child by giving yourself to God and believing in Him. You are to live in Him in the same way. The apostle Paul wrote, "Since you have accepted Christ Jesus as Lord, live in union with him" (Colossians 2:6).

Come As You Are

Some people feel that they are on trial and must prove to the Lord that they have changed before they can receive His blessing. But they may receive the blessing right now. They must have His grace, the Spirit of Christ, to help them overcome their weaknesses. Without it they cannot fight against sin.

Jesus loves to have us come to Him just as we are, sinful, helpless, and needy. We may come, foolish and weak as we are, and fall at His feet in sorrow for sin. It is His glory to put His arms of love around us, heal our wounds, and make us clean.

Thousands believe that Jesus pardons other people, but not them. They do no believe what God says. But every person who truly repents can know for himself that God freely pardons every one of his sins.

Do not fear. God's promises are meant for you. They are for every person who is sorry for his sins. Christ sends angels to bring strength and grace to every believing person. Even the most sinful persons can be strong, pure, and righteous by accepting Jesus, who died for them. Christ is waiting to take away our sin-soiled clothes, and to put on us the clean, white clothes of righteousness. He wants us to live and not die.

God does not treat us the way people treat each other. He thinks of us with love, mercy, and pity. He says, "Let the wicked leave their way of life and change their way of thinking. Let them turn to the Lord, our God; for he is merciful and quick to forgive" (Isaiah 55:7). "I have swept your sins away like a cloud. Come back to me: I am the one who saves you" (Isaiah 44:22).

Don't Entertain Any Doubts

The Lord says, "I do not want anyone to die . . . Turn away from your sins and live" (Ezekiel 18:32). Satan tries to keep you from believing the blessed promises of God. He wants to take away from you every bit of hope and every ray of light. But you must not let him do this. Do not listen to Satan. Say to him, "Jesus died so that I could live. He loves me and does not want me to die. I have a loving heavenly Father. Even though I have turned form His love and wasted His blessings, I will go to my Father. I will say, 'I have sinned against Heaven and against You. I am no longer worthy to be called Your son. Treat me as one of Your hired workers.' "

Jesus told the story of a son who had left home and how he was received when he decided to come back. "He was still a long way from home when his father saw him; his heart was filled with pity, and he ran, threw his arms around his son, and kissed him" (Luke 15:20).

This is a beautiful story, but it cannot fully tell of the heavenly Father's love and pity. The Lord said through His prophet, "I have always loved you, so I continue to show you my constant love" (Jeremiah 31:3). The Father is hoping for the sinner's return even while the sinner is far away wasting his life and money in a strange country. When a person feels a desire to return to God, this is God's Spirit calling, trying to bring the sinner to the Father's heart of love.

With the wonderful promises of the Bible before you, how can you doubt? How can you think that Jesus will not welcome the sinner who wants to turn from his sins? Put away such thoughts! Nothing can hurt you more than believing such an idea about our heavenly Father.

The Father hates sin, but He loves the sinner. He gave Himself when He gave Christ that all who would believe might be saved. He wanted them to be blessed forever in his kingdom of glory.

What stronger or more loving words could He use to tell us how much He loves us? He said, "Can a woman forget her own baby and not love the child she bore? Even if a mother should forget her child, I will never forget you" (Isaiah 49:15).

Look up to Jesus if you have doubts and fears. He lives to ask God to forgive your sins. Thank God for the gift of His dear Son. Pray that His death for you will not be useless. The Spirit invites you today. Come with your whole heart to Jesus and receive His blessing.

Read His promises. Remember that they tell of His love and pity, which are stronger than words can tell. God's great heart of infinite love turns to the sinner with never-ending pity. "By the blood of Christ we are set free, that is, our sins are forgiven" (Ephesians 1:7).

Believe that God is your helper. He wants to change your life, to make it like His perfect life. Come close to Him as you confess your sins and repent, and He will come close to you with mercy and forgiveness.

Chapter 10
Scars Don't Bleed

"There is something beautiful about all scars of whatever nature. A scar means the hurt is over, the wound is closed and healed, done with."

Those are the words of American novelist, short story writer and essayist, Harry Crews (b. 1935). The quote captures the self-evident truth that although scars can be embarrassing and ugly, they evidence that the wounds that were once fresh and painful have been healed. And because the wounds are healed, the scars they leave behind cannot bleed.

In fact, the telling evidence that the wounds have been fully healed is that they don't hurt anymore. The scars become marks of our identity and we even show off the marks to tell our stories. When our wounds are healed, we act as little children and lovers, whose attitude towards scars has been aptly stated by Leonard Cohen: "Children show scars like medals. Lovers use them as secrets to reveal."

What is the evidence that our wounds of sin have been healed? What is the proof that the person, who used to make wrong choices in life, has now been changed? And what is the evidence that a person is now a true Christian?

This chapter argues that the real test of a changed life is how we now live our lives after our sins have been forgiven. The choices we make after receiving healing from our spiritual wounds testify to whether or not we have been truly changed.[1]

Becoming A New Person

"Anyone who is jointed to Christ is a new being; the old is gone, the new has come" (2 Corinthians 5:17).

A person may not be able to tell the exact time or place when he gave his heart to God. He may not see the steps that brought him to Christ. But this does not prove that he is not a child of God. Christ said to Nicodemus, "The wind blows wherever it wishes; you hear the sound it makes, but you do not know where it comes from or where it is going. It is like that with everyone who is born of the Spirit" (John 3:8).

We cannot see the wind, but we can see what it does. We cannot see the Spirit of God as he works on the heart, but His power brings us new life. That power creates a new person in the image of God. Although we cannot see or hear the working of the Spirit, we can see what he has done.

Our Lives Will Show Change

If our hearts have been changed by the Spirit of God, our lives will show the change. We cannot change our hearts or make our characters like God's. We must not trust in our own strength or believe that our good deeds will save us. But our lives will show whether we have the grace of God in our hearts. It will change our characters, our habits, and the way we live. Other people will see the difference between what we used to be and what we now are.

The character is not shown by one good deed or even a bad one. The character is shown by the way we speak and act day after day.

It is true that we may act in the right way without the power of God. We may do good so that other people will think well of us. We may even avoid evil because we want to look right in the sight of our friends. Even a selfish person may give to a good cause, or help the needy. How can we know, then, whose side we are on?

How Can We Tell?

Who owns our hearts? Whom are we thinking about? Whom do we love to talk about? Who has our warmest love and our best work? If we are Christ's, we think often about Him, and our kindest thoughts are of Him. We have laid at his feet all we have and are. We want to be like Him and have His Spirit in us. We desire to follow His way and to please Him in everything.

If we become new persons in Christ Jesus, we will have the fruits of the Spirit in our lives. They are "love, joy, peace, patience, kindness, goodness, faithfulness, humility, and self-control" (Galatians 5:22,23). Followers of Christ will no longer act as they did before. They will follow by faith in Christ's footsteps. They will show His character and be pure, just as He is pure.

Those who follow Christ will love the things they used to hate. They will hate the things they used to love. The proud will become humble. The foolish will become wise. Those who used to get drunk will stay sober. Impure people will become pure. Those who loved the proud fashions of the word will lay them aside.

Christians will not try to gain attention by the things they wear. "Instead, your beauty should consist of your true inner self, the ageless beauty of a gentle and quiet spirit, which is the greatest value in God's sight" (1Peter 3:4).

True repentance changes a person. The sinner will confess his sins and return that he has stolen. He will love God and other people. When the sinner does these things, he will know that he has passed from death into life.

When we come to Christ and accept His pardon and grace, love develops in our hearts. Our work does not seem hard, and what God asks us to do becomes a pleasure. The path that used to be dark is made bright by rays from the Sun of Righteousness.

The beauty of Christ's character will be seen in His followers. Christ was delighted to do what His Father asked. Love to God was the guiding power in our Saviour's life. Love made all His acts kind and beautiful.

Love comes from God. It cannot come from sinful hearts. It is found only in hearts where Jesus lives. "We love because God first loved us" (1John 4:19). In hearts made new by God's grace, love is the guiding power. Love changes our characters, rules our feelings, and controls our desires. It drives out hate and helps us be true to those we love. God's love in our hearts sweetens our lives and has a good influence on everyone around us.

Two Mistakes to Avoid

Children of God need to guard against two mistakes in thinking. People who have just started to trust God especially need to watch for these. The first, which has already been explained, is the mistake of trusting our good works to bring ourselves to God. If we try to become holy by obeying the law in our own strength, we will find it impossible. Everything we do without Christ is spoiled by selfishness and sin. Only the grace of Christ, tough faith, can make us holy.

The second mistake is just as dangerous. It is the idea that we do not need to keep the law of God when we believe in Christ. Since the grace of God is received through faith alone, some people think that what they do has nothing to do with their redemption.

The Bible teaches that obedience is more than just doing right. It is more than doing what we are told to do. Obedience is the service of love. God's law shows us what He is like. Love is the very center of the law. God's government in heaven and on earth is built on His law of love.

Will not the law of God be carried out in our lives if we are like Him? When love is in our hearts and when we become like our Creator, God keeps His promise: "I will put my laws in their hearts and write them on their minds" (Hebrews 10:16).

If the law is written in the heart, will it not shape the life? Obedience is a true sign of love. It also is the sign that we are followers of God. The Bible says, "our love for God means that we obey his commands." "If we say that we know him, but do not obey his commands, we are liars and there is no truth in us" (1John 5:3, 2:4). Through faith, and faith alone, we share the grace of Christ. And grace makes it possible for us to obey His law.

We do not earn salvation by obeying God's law. Salvation is God's free gift, and we receive it by faith. But obedience is the fruit of faith. "You know that Christ appeared in order to take away sins, and that there is no sin in him. So everyone who lives in union with Christ does not continue to sin; but whoever continues to sin has never seen him or known him" (1John 3:5,6). This is the true test.

The True Test of Being Changed

When we live in Christ and His love lives in us, our feelings and our thought will agree with what His holy law shows us God wants us to do. "Let no one deceive you, my children! Whoever does what is right is righteous, just as Christ is righteous" (verse 7). God's holy ten-commandment law given to Israel on Sinai tells us what righteousness is.

A faith in Christ which teaches that we do not need o obey God is not true faith. It is teaching something that is not true. "For it is by God's grace that you have been saved through faith" (Ephesians 2:8). "Even so faith, if it hath not works, is dead" (James 2:17, KJV). Jesus said of Himself before He came to earth, "How I love to do your will, my God! I keep your teaching in my heart" (Psalm 40:8).

Before Jesus returned to heaven after being on earth, He said, "I have obeyed my Father's commands and remain in his love" (John 15:10). The Bible says, "If we obey God's commands, then we are sure that we know him." "If we say that we remain in union with God, we should live just as Jesus Christ did" (1 John 2:3, 6). "For Christ himself suffered for you and left you an example, so that you would follow in his steps" (I Peter 2:21).

The plan by which God gives us eternal life has always been the same. It is still the same as it was in the Garden of Eden before the Adam and Eve sinned. God gives eternal life to those who obey His law perfectly, to those who have perfect righteousness.

Eternal life cannot be given by any other plan, for then the happiness of all creation would be in danger. Sin would go on forever. Suffering and unhappiness would never end.

It was possible for Adam before he sinned to form a righteous character by obeying God's law. But Adam failed to do this. Because of his sin, we are all sinners, and we cannot make ourselves righteous. Because we are sinful and unholy, we cannot perfectly obey God's law. We have no righteousness of our own to do what God's law requires.

But Christ has made a way of escape for us. He lived on earth, facing the same kind of trials and temptations we have to face. He lived a sinless life. He died for us, and now He offers to take our sins and give us His righteousness.

We may give ourselves to Him and accept Him as our Saviour. Then, no matter how sinful our lives have been, we are counted as being righteous because of Him. Christ's character will stand in the place of our characters. We are accepted by God just as if we had not sinned.

More than this, Christ changes our hearts. He lives in our hearts by faith. We are to keep Him in our hearts by faith and let Him guide all our choices. As long as we do this, He will work in us and we will do what pleases Him. We may then say, "This life that I live now, I live by faith in the Son of God, who loved me and gave his life for me" (Galatians 2:20).

Jesus said to His disciples, "The words you will speak will not be yours; they will come from the Spirit of your Father speaking through you" (Matthew 10:20). Then, with Christ working in us, we will act as He would act and do His good works. Our lives would show obedience, the works of righteousness.

So you see, we have nothing to be proud of and no reason to praise ourselves. Our only hope is in the righteousness of Christ, which God counts as ours, and in that righteousness His Spirit works out in us and through us.

True and False Faith

We should understand the true meaning of faith. When we believe what we already know is true, we are not showing faith. We know God lives. We believe in His power. We know His word is true. Even Satan and his angels know and believe these things. The Bible says that "the devils also believe, and tremble" (James 2:19, KJV). But this is not faith.

We have faith when we not only believe God's Word but ask Him to guide all our choices. We show our faith when we give our hearts to Him and love Him. This kind of faith works by love and makes us pure. It changes us until we become like Him.

If our hearts have not been made new by God, we fight against God's law and do not obey it. But our new hearts delight in the holy laws. We can say with David, "How I love your law. I think about it all day long" (Psalm 119:97). And the righteousness of the law is worked into the lives of people who "live in union with Christ" (Romans 8:1).

Don't Be Discouraged by Your Shortcomings

Some people know that God has pardoned their sins, and they really want to be His children. But they know that their characters are not perfect and their lives have many faults. Because of this they doubt that the Holy Spirit has made their hearts new.

To such people I would say, "Do not be discouraged and lose hope. We shall often have to bow down and weep at the feet of Jesus because we make mistakes and are not perfect. Yet we are not to give up. God does not turn away from us even if we are overcome by the enemy. He does not leave us alone."

Christ is at the right hand of God. He is asking His Father to forgive us. John, the greatly loved disciple wrote, "I am writing this to you, my children, so that you will not sin; but if anyone does sin, we have someone who pleads with the Father on our behalf—Jesus Christ, the righteous one" (1 John 2:1).

We must not forget these words of Christ: "The Father himself loves you" (John 16:27). He desires to bring us back to Himself. He wants to see His own purity and holiness reflected in us. If we will give ourselves to Him until Jesus comes, He will continue the good work He has begun in us.

We must pray with great desire. We must believe more fully. As we begin to lose faith in our own power, let us trust the power of our Redeemer. Let us praise Him who is the light of our lives.

The closer we come to Jesus, the more faults we will see in our lives. We will see our faults more clearly as we compare our sinful selves with the perfect Saviour. This will show that Satan's false ideas are losing their power over us and that the life-giving Spirit of God is leading us.

Deep love for Jesus cannot live in our hearts if we do not know we are sinful. If we are changed by the grace of Christ, we will admire the Saviour's holy character. If we do not see that we are sinful, this shows that we have never seen the beauty and perfection of Christ.

The less we find to admire in ourselves, the more we shall see to admire in Christ's infinite purity and beauty. When we see how sinful we are, we turn to Him who can pardon. When we see that we have no power, we reach out after Christ. Then Christ comes with power to help.

Our sense of need drives us to the Saviour and the Word of God. The more we see of His beautiful character, the more we shall become like Him.

Endnote

1. Our presentation in this chapter is actually chapter 7 of the must-read devotional classic *Steps to Jesus.* It is titled there "The Test of Discipleship." I will adopt the title "Becoming A New Person." Perceptive readers will discover that the titles I've chosen in chapters 6 to 10 of this book for the materials from *Steps to Jesus* are actually the chapter titles from *Peace Above the Storm: Freedom from Worry, Guilt and Fear* (Nampa, Idaho: Pacific Press, 1994). The text for *Peace Above the Storm* is actually E. G. White's *Steps to Christ.*

PART III

LIVING WITH THE UGLY SCARS

(Living With the Consequences of Wrong Choices)

"The optimist already sees the scar over the wound; the pessimist still sees the wound underneath the scar"
—Ernst Schroder

"And one shall say unto him, What are these wounds in thine hands? Then he shall answer, Those with which I was wounded in the house of my friends."
(Zechariah 13:6; KJV).

"I believe the single most significant decision I can make on a day-to-day basis is my choice of attitude. It is more important than my past, my education, my bankroll, my successes or failures, fame or pain, what other people think of me or say about me, my circumstances, or my position. Attitude keeps me going or cripples my progress. It alone fuels my fire or assaults my hope. When my attitudes are right, there is no barrier too high, no valley too deep, no dream too extreme, no challenge too great for me."
—Charles R. Swindol

Chapter 11
Bleeding Scars

Not all wounds are self-inflicted. Some are caused by the decisions and actions of others. The injury from such wounds can be very painful—especially if the wounds are deep and were deliberately inflicted upon us by either our friends or enemies.

Many of us are still hurting from the hurt caused by people who, at one time or the other, were near or dear to us—perhaps a relative, classmate, co-worker, parent, child, husband, or wife. Perhaps we have been seriously wounded in church. We have been hurt, betrayed, defrauded, humiliated, violated, or wounded by a church member, elder, Sabbath school teacher, or pastor.

Those of us who have been thus wounded cannot bring ourselves to forgive those who inflicted the wounds upon us. We are pained, bitter, and angry at what happened to us and at those who caused it. We feel justified to withhold forgiveness.

But as painful as our wounds may be, there is another wound which is worse. *The worst wounds ever inflicted upon us are those we inflict upon ourselves by our decision not to forgive our wound-ers.* I call the sin of not forgiving—or unforgiveness—"suicidal wounds."

The Bible questions the legitimacy of the healing of people who claim to have experienced God's forgiveness and yet still cherish an unforgiving spirit towards their wound-ers. I refer to the spot of their supposed healing as "bleeding scars." For real scars do *not* bleed.

Suicidal Wounds and Bleeding Scars

Both forgiveness and unforgiveness are choices we make. The word *forgiveness* is a legal term used 143 times in the New Testament. It means "to release a person from an obligation." When used in financial contexts, it carries the idea of canceling a debt. The implication is inescapable: Forgiveness always involves a choice. Thus, unforgiveness is also a choice. As such, it also has consequences.

Unforgiveness is as dangerous as cancer. It eats away at us from the inside. It deprives us of our peace of mind, it holds us in perpetual bondage to the person who wounded us, and the Bible makes it clear that those who do not forgive will themselves not be forgiven by God (Matthew 6:14-15). Thus, to the extent that we choose not to forgive—not to let go of—something that is eating us up, we commit spiritual suicide.

What, then, should we do when we find it very difficult to forgive those who have deliberately wounded us? How do we heal our suicidal wounds? How can we be set free from the sin of our unforgiveness? The answer to these questions involve a painful choice. But it is a choice that sets us free and secures our own forgiveness.

Case Histories

It is said that the most *forgiven* people should be the most *forgiving* people. And yet, this is easier said than done. Some of us are too hurt to forgive those who have wounded us. Let me illustrate what I mean with the following concrete examples that have come to my notice. I have personalized each example so that you can ask yourself this specific question: "Why should I and how can I forgive this particular person and forget what they have done to me?"

- Your closest friend wants your position; she lies and spreads false rumors about you, ruining your good reputation, and takes your position or job. After you've endured seven years of humiliation, loss, and pain that resulted in a severe emotional breakdown and rehabilitation at a mental institution, your friend comes back to you quietly, saying she is sorry.
- Your employee steals thousands of your company's money and runs away from the law by fleeing to a foreign country. In the far-away country, he squanders the thousands of dollars, and after three years he comes back, saying he is sorry.
- Your brother has been killed by a hit-and-run driver, who happens to be your neighbor. But the perpetrator is unrepentant, lies

about it, and wants you to treat him as though he wasn't responsible for the death of your brother.

- Your family friend from another ethnic group has an affair with your otherwise faithful wife. She becomes pregnant and wants you to take her back, forgive the other man involved, and accept the child (with obvious external characteristics of another race) as your very own.
- In a racial/tribal conflict, your fellow church member leads a mob of gangsters (vigilantes) to kill your husband and children. They leave you for dead after you have sustained severe wounds and fallen unconscious. The assailants then proceed to loot the belongings of your family. After being miraculously rescued and after months of hospital care, you recover from your comatose condition. Then in a marketplace, you come face to face with the church member who led the murderers to your home. Fearing mob-justice, your assailant pleads for forgiveness.

Why Must We Forgive and Forget?

How should we deal with the anger, pain, and hurt resulting from the real situations mentioned above? How should we treat that person who has seriously hurt us, and yet comes back claiming he is sorry? What about the ones who still remain unrepentant? Are we really expected to forgive them also?

For those whose wounds are still fresh, these questions are not theoretical ones. Even when we say we have forgiven, we sometimes don't want to have anything to do with those who have hurt us. So I ask again, why must we let go our hurt and bitterness for the joy of reconciliation and peace? Why must we forgive and forget?

The Bible offers us several reasons why we should forgive those who have wronged us. I will summarize these at the end of this chapter. However, in the main body of this chapter, I will concentrate on what I consider to be the most compelling reason why we must forgive and forget—namely, *for Christ's sake.* This motivation is remarkably captured in a story found in the ninth chapter of the second book of Samuel.

If you want to know why you have to forgive and show kindness to the person who has terribly hurt you, look at how King David treated Mephibosheth, the grandson of Saul, and why he did so. Then you will get a glimpse into the heart of God, and this will challenge you to forgive—even your worst enemy.

David and Mephibosheth

A Frantic Quest. 2 Samuel 9 begins with a frantic question from King David: "Is there still anyone who is left of the house of Saul, that I may show him kindness for Jonathan's sake?" (v. 1) Apparently King David had been searching for someone from the household of his worst enemy Saul. The king wants to show kindness to Saul's descendants "for Jonathan's sake." Though there seems to be no meaningful response to his quest, David does not give up.

In verse 3, he repeats the question and explains the nature of kindness he wants to bestow on such a person: "Then the king said, 'Is there not still someone of the house of Saul, to whom I may show the kindness of God?'"

What David does not know is that there is only one descendant of Saul left. He is a crippled young man named Mephibosheth, the son of Jonathan and the grandson of King Saul. At the time of David's inquiry, Mephibosheth is married and living in exile in a far-away town called Lo-debar.

The Fall, Escape, and Exile. The Bible offers only a brief account of how he has become crippled. One day, when Mephibosheth was only five years old, word reached the palace that in the war between the Israelites and the Philistines at Jezreel, King Saul had been killed. Prince Jonathan had also been killed. In fact, virtually all of Saul's children and grandchildren had been wiped out. Saul's very large family (cf. 1 Chronicles 8:33), enough to replenish a country, was virtually wiped out literally overnight.

One can only imagine how the National Security Council in Saul's day might have handled this crisis. I suspect that they quickly convened an emergency session in the palace to decide what to do. Who is asked to hold the reins? What should they do, especially given the fact that David and his band of soldiers are in the hills and might take advantage of the tragedy by taking over power?

With the sudden change of mood in the palace, Mephibosheth no doubt, feels that something is wrong. Perhaps in apprehension or fear, he cries for his daddy and grandpa. Yet no one is ready to disclose the facts to this five-year-old boy—no one, except the royal nurse.

I can almost hear the nurse explaining to Mephibosheth: "Daddy and Grandpa cannot come home tonight because they went to fight so you could become the next king of Israel . . . But we have to leave the palace immediately, if we are to avoid being killed by David and his men."

No doubt Mephibosheth can't understand why David would want to kill him. Is not David his daddy's best friend? The royal nurse explains: "David hates you; he wants to kill you and take the kingdom that belongs to your father and grandfather. He hates you because your grandfather Saul hated him and tried to kill him more than once. Now that your dad and grandpa are dead, David will seek revenge by killing you. . . . We have to leave right away."

We don't really know what happened in the palace. All we know for sure is what the Bible says in 2 Samuel 4:4: "Jonathan, Saul's son, had a son who was lame in his feet. He was five years old when the news about Saul and Jonathan came from Jezreel; and his nurse took him up and fled. And it happened, as she made haste to flee, that he fell and became lame. His name was Mephibosheth."

Apparently in the nurse's haste to flee with Mephibosheth, he fell, perhaps injuring his spinal cord so that he is paralyzed or crippled for life. Utilizing maximum secrecy, and using (perhaps) a fake passport and ID documents, Mephibosheth was sent into exile in Lo-debar.

I can imagine the nurse charging him never to disclose his true identity, but telling him that one day at the appropriate time he would be brought back into Israel to claim his rightful place on the throne. Until that time, he was to flee for his life whenever he hears that David and his men are looking for him.

Thus, from the age of five, Mephibosheth is brainwashed into believing that David hated him and wanted to do him harm. For the remainder of his life, Mephibosheth lived in obscurity, blaming and hating David for all the misfortunes of his life.

A Long Search. Meanwhile back in Israel, King David was on the throne. Since his enthronement, he has had one overriding concern. It is not just consolidating his power, but offering special honor to the descendants of his archenemy, Saul.

David's search for Mephibosheth took several years, a great while after his accession to the throne. Mephibosheth, five years old when Saul dies, has a son when he is found (2 Samuel 9:12). If we assume that he is 30 years old when he is married and has his son a year afterwards, it takes at least 25 years for David to find Mephibosheth.

For 25 long years the king is thinking, inquiring, and searching for this lost, crippled son of his friend! If David lived in our day, I can imagine him using all the intelligence apparatus—such as the United State's CIA and FBI, the UK's MI3 and Scotland Yard, the Israeli Mossad, the Interpol, and others—to look for Mephibosheth.

Face to Face Encounter. At long last, the Bible tells us, David's security agents identify Ziba, a former employee of King Saul, who help to locate the whereabouts of Mephibosheth (cf. 2 Samuel 9:3-5). The Bible's account of the meeting of Mephibosheth and David reveals how hatred is swallowed by love and fear by trust. It is worth reading it in its entirety:

> Now when Mephibosheth the son of Jonathan, the son of Saul, had come to David, he fell on his face and prostrated himself. Then David said, "Mephibosheth?" And he answered, "Here is your servant!"
>
> So David said to him, "Do not fear, for I will surely show you kindness for Jonathan your father's sake, and will restore to you all the land of Saul your grandfather; and you shall eat bread at my table continually."
>
> Then he bowed himself, and said, "What is your servant, that you should look upon such a dead dog as I?"
>
> And the king called to Ziba, Saul's servant, and said to him,

> "I have given to your master's son all that belonged to Saul and to all his house. You therefore, and your sons and your servants, shall work the land for him, and you shall bring in the harvest, that your master's son may have food to eat. But Mephibosheth your master's son shall eat bread at my table always." Now Ziba had fifteen sons and twenty servants.
>
> Then Ziba said to the king, "According to all that my lord the king has commanded his servant, so will your servant do."
>
> "As for Mephibosheth," said the king, "he shall eat at my table like one of the king's sons." Mephibosheth had a young son whose name was Micha. And all who dwelt in the house of Ziba were servants of Mephibosheth.
>
> So Mephibosheth dwelt in Jerusalem, for he ate continually at the king's table. And he was lame in both his feet (2 Samuel 9:6-13).

In case you missed it, "for Jonathan's sake," David took his avowed enemy, restored to him the estate of his grandfather Saul, allowed him to live with him in the palace, and treated him like one of his own sons! Though Mephibosheth is lame and unsightly, and did not seem to have any great fitness for service, yet, for his good father's sake, David took him to be one of his family—even risking a future usurpation!

The Gospel of Salvation

This account of David's treatment of Mephibosheth teaches many important lessons. First, it is one of the greatest illustrations of the gospel. It reveals something about the riches of God's grace. In this real story, David represents God the Father, sitting on His throne and seeking to show kindness to us sinners. Though we hate Him, misconstrue His intentions and plans towards us, deny Him, and fail Him over and over again, He still loves us and is ever searching for us to save us. "Behold what manner of love the Father has bestowed on us, that we should be called children of God!" (1 John 3:1).

Mephibosheth represents us—lost humanity, crippled by sin. Like

Saul's grandson, we also fell—not in a palace, but in a garden called Eden (Genesis 3). Because of the Fall, we cannot walk straight, think straight, talk straight, nor do anything straight. We hate God, distrust Him, and disbelieve His Word. Far away from the Father's home, we live in the obscurity and shadow of sin. The Bible says, "all have sinned, and come short of the glory of God" (Romans 3:23).

Though created in the image of God and, hence, from the Royal family, we are so degraded in sin that we feel like we are "dead dogs." Indeed, we deserve death, for "the wages of sin is death" (Rom 6:23a). Notice, however, that this text does not end there. It continues: "but the gift of God is eternal life through Jesus Christ our Lord" (Romans 6:23b).

Jonathan represents our Lord Jesus Christ. The only way we Mephibosheths can be saved is through Him. The name Jonathan means "gift of God." It is not surprising that the greatest gift God has given humanity is His Son. "For God so loved the world that He *gave* His only begotten Son, that whoever believes in Him should not perish but have everlasting life" (John 3:16; emphasis mine).

Thus, any time we read the phrase "for Jonathan's sake" in the 2 Samuel 9 account, it really means "for Christ's sake." The only reason why God shows kindness to us, pardoning us of our sins and making us His sons and daughters, is for Christ's sake. "I write to you, little children, because your sins are forgiven you *for His name's sake*" (1 John 2:12; emphasis mine).

It is for Christ's sake that we Mephibosheths are adopted as sons and daughters of God (John 1:12). And it is also for Christ's sake that we have the assurance of eternal life, the promise of His indwelling Spirit and the hope of living forever with God (1 John 5:13; cf. Rom 8:14-39).

Our Ethical Obligation to Others

The second lesson we learn from the account of David's treatment of Mephibosheth is our ethical obligation to others. For some 25 long years, King David frantically searched for a descendant of his enemy in order to show kindness to him. Why is David so eager to show kindness?

The answer is found in 1 Samuel 20:11-17. There we read that David made a promise to Jonathan that one day he (David) would pay back the kindness he himself has received from Jonathan. David could satisfy his conscience by saying Jonathan is dead or that Mephibosheth hasn't requested help. But no. The king inquired and searched until he found Mephibosheth.

Though Mephibosheth had, apparently, never requested help, though he had apparently been taught to hate David, and thus doesn't deserve help, David showed kindness to him "for Jonathan's sake." Mephibosheth received favor on account of the merit of Jonathan. This is grace at work. Hence for 25 years the king is thinking, inquiring, and searching for this lost, crippled son!

We may also owe a debt to someone, and it is our moral duty to look for that person and do kindness to him or her. How long have you been searching for that one person to whom you owe a debt: a grade school teacher, nurse, aunt, grandmother, pastor, or friend?

Is there a promise you have long neglected? Now is the time to make good on it. Better late than never!

The Motivation to Forgive

The third lesson we can learn from David's treatment of Mephibosheth is the motivation to forgive. Why does David show kindness to Mephibosheth, making him one of the king's sons and allowing him to eat from then on at the king's table? Why does he adopt as his son one who hates him, the one who may potentially work to undermine and usurp his government? Why does David forgive the grandchild of his avowed enemy?

The answer is twice repeated in the 2 Samuel 9 passage: "For Jonathan's sake" (v. 1); "For Jonathan your father's sake" (v. 7).

In the phrase "for Jonathan's sake," we find the most compelling motivation to forgive others. As we mentioned earlier, this phrase means "for Christ's sake." In other words, if we are looking for a reason to forgive and forget the ills we have suffered at the hands of others, the answer lies in what Jesus, our divine Jonathan, has done for us. Those who understand the price Christ paid on Calvary for their sins will not stubbornly withhold forgiveness from those who have hurt them.

This is why the most forgiven person ought to be the most *forgiving* individual. Though it hurts to forgive, the Bible urges us—for Christ's sake—to do the unthinkable. Observe how often the expression "for Christ's sake" appears in the New Testament (King James Version, KJV):

1. *We must forgive one another for Christ's sake:* "And be ye kind one to another, tenderhearted, forgiving one another, even as God *for Christ's sake* hath forgiven you" (Ephesians 4:32).
2. *We must pray for one another for Christ's sake:* "*For* the Lord Jesus *Christ's sake,* and for the love of the Spirit, that ye strive together with me in your prayers to God for me" (Romans 15:30).
3. *We must become fools in the eyes of others and be despised for Christ's sake:* "We are fools *for Christ's sake;* but ye are wise in Christ; we are weak, but ye are strong; ye are honourable, but we are despised" (1 Corinthians 4:10).
4. *We must preach the truth and be true servants of God for Christ's sake:* "For we preach not ourselves, but Christ Jesus the Lord; and ourselves your servants *for Jesus' sake*" (2 Corinthians 4:5).
5. *We must patiently endure the trials of life for Christ's sake:* "Therefore I take pleasure in infirmities, in reproaches, in necessities, in persecutions, in distresses *for Christ's sake:* for when I am weak, then am I strong" (2 Corinthians 12:10).
6. *We must be willing to suffer for Christ's sake:* "For unto you it is given in the behalf of Christ, not only to believe on him, but also to suffer *for his sake*" (Philippians 1:29).
7. *We must suffer persecution for Christ's (church's) sake:* "Who now rejoice in my sufferings for you, and fill up that which is behind of the afflictions of Christ in my flesh *for his body's sake,* which is the church" (Colossians 1:24).
8. *We must be willing to die for Christ's sake:* "For we which live are always delivered unto death *for Jesus' sake,* that the life also of Jesus might be made manifest in our mortal flesh" (2 Corinthians 4:11).
9. *We must submit to good ordinances of those in power for Christ's sake:*

"Submit yourselves to every ordinance of man *for the Lord's sake:* whether it be to the king, as supreme" (1 Peter 2:13).

10. *The Lord will richly bless and save us if we endure unto the end for Christ's sake:* "Blessed are ye, when men shall revile you, and persecute you, and shall say all manner of evil against you falsely, *for my sake*" (Matthew 5:11; cf. Luke 6:22). "And ye shall be hated of all men *for my name's sake:* but he that shall endure unto the end, the same shall be saved" (Mark 13:13).

It is obvious from the above passages that the most compelling reason to do the right thing, including forgiving those who have hurt us, is "for Christ's sake." The more we understand the amazing grace of God's forgiveness, the more our motivation to forgive others. The basis and motivation to forgive others is what Christ has done for us.

What It Means to Forgive & Forget

Forgiveness is a choice. It is a conscious decision of the mind and heart to freely remit the offense of another, regardless of the cost. Unfortunately, many of us have difficulty forgiving others because we confuse forgiveness with what it is not. For example:

Forgiveness is not excusing the wrong conduct of others. Excusing says, "That's OK," and seems to suggest that what a person did wasn't really wrong or that he or she couldn't help it. But forgiveness is not excusing or justifying the wrong conduct of a person.

On the contrary, the very nature of forgiveness suggests that what a person did was wrong and inexcusable. Covering up sin (which is what excusing is) cannot bring about forgiveness. The Bible says, "He who covers his sins will not prosper, but whoever confesses and forsakes them will have mercy" (Proverbs 28:13). True forgiveness honestly acknowledges that what a person did to us is wrong, but chooses, by the grace of God, to let go.

Forgiveness is not weakness. Sometimes, we think that when we forgive others, it is a sign of our weakness or cowardice. And who wants to be perceived as an easy pushover or a door mat?

The truth, however, is that forgiveness is never borne out of weakness, but rather from a position of strength and power. It takes a person who is strong in patience and inner strength to forgive. When God chooses to forgive us, it is not because He is powerless. Only those with resolute convictions and sterling character can truly forgive. On the other hand, as long as we choose not to forgive, we become the slaves of those who have hurt us.

Forgiveness is not forgetting. Forgetting is to lose the remembrance or recollection of something. It is a *passive* process in which the passing of time causes a thing to fade from memory. Forgiving, however, is not the result of amnesia. Instead, it is an *active* process in which a person makes a conscious choice not to mention, recount, or think about the injury one has suffered from another.

When God says He will "I will not remember your sins" (Isaiah 43:25), it does not mean He *cannot* remember our sins, but that He will *not* remember them. It is a conscious choice on His part not to reckon those sins against us nor take action on them. The good news, however, is that when we make a conscious decision to forgive and to stop dwelling on the offense of others, the Lord works a miracle in us so that the hurts we have suffered lose their bite—to the extent that the painful memories fade away.

Forgiveness is not a feeling—a fleeting emotional experience. It is conscious choice, *an act of the will.* Forgiveness is a decision not to think, talk about, or be influenced by the ill-conduct of another.

Two Greek words are often translated as "forgive." The first, *aphiemi,* means to let go, release, or remit. It is a term used to describe the full payment or cancellation of a debt (cf. Matthew 6:12; 18:27, 32). The other word is *charizomai,* which means to bestow favor freely or unconditionally. This term suggests that forgiveness is an act of grace. It is undeserved and cannot be earned.[1] Both terms imply that the one doing the forgiving suffers some loss or pain. This is what happened on Calvary when our Lord Jesus Christ chose to suffer and die, in order to secure our forgiveness.[2]

Forgiveness is not a feel-good experience. The choice to let go really hurts. Still one *chooses* to pay the price. Though forgiveness is not a feeling, and though the decision to forgive hurts, the good news is that this conscious act of the will to forgive also brings about changes in our feelings. We experience a certain peace and joy for doing God's will.

So Why Forgive and Forget?

Our willingness or unwillingness to forgive reveals much about us. Any time we cherish an unforgiving attitude, stubbornly withholding forgiveness from others, let us remember the following facts:

Our unforgiving spirit reveals how we want God to treat us. When we are very hurt, we often say things like, "I will never forgive him" or that "though I will forgive, I will never forget what he did to me." Others say, "I will always stay away or not talk to her again as long as I live." What would happen if God applied the Golden Rule and treated us the same way we treat others? (The Golden Rule, by the way, says in essence, "Do unto others what you want to be done unto you"; see Matthew 7:12; Luke 6:31).

How would you feel if, after confessing your sins to the Lord, you hear a voice from heaven saying, "I have forgiven you, but I just don't want to have anything to do with you again"? Or what if the Lord spoke to you audibly: "I have forgiven you, but I will never forget what you did to me." I don't think many of would feel secure in that kind of divine forgiveness.

The Scriptures urge us to forgive others, just as God has forgiven us. The Lord has freely forgiven us. We also must do likewise for others. "And be ye kind one to another, tenderhearted, forgiving one another, *even as God for Christ's sake hath forgiven you*" (Ephesians 4:32; KJV). "Forbearing one another, and forgiving one another, if any man have a quarrel against any: *even as Christ forgave you, so also do ye*" (Colossians 3:13; KJV).

Our unforgiving spirit reveals our lack of appreciation of God's forgiveness. A forgiven Christian is always forgiving. If we don't forgive others, it is an indication that we don't value Christ's forgiveness. This fact is remarkably captured in Christ's parable of the two debtors in Matthew 18:21-35. In that story, one servant owes a king a substantial debt. When the king threatens to sell the servant and his family to pay the debt, the servant pleads for mercy. The king is "moved with compassion," has mercy on him and forgives him the debt (v. 27).

Moments later, the forgiven servant sees a fellow servant who owes him a much smaller debt. When he asks for payment, the man asks for time to do so. But the forgiven servant refuses and "went and threw him into prison till he should pay the debt" (v. 30). When the king hears about this, he summons the forgiven (but now unforgiving) servant and says: "You wicked servant! I forgave you all that debt because you begged me. Should you not also have had compassion on your fellow servant, just as I had pity on you?" (vv. 32-33) In his anger, the king delivers the unforgiving debtor to the jailors.

Jesus concludes the parable with these sobering words: "So My heavenly Father also will do to you if each of you, *from his heart, does not forgive his brother his trespasses*" (Matthew 18:35). You see, forgiveness is at the heart of the gospel, and the new birth is nothing other than divine forgiveness doing its life-changing work in the life of the repentant sinner. Those who refuse to forgive put in jeopardy their own forgiven status.

Our unforgiving spirit reveals whether or not we shall receive and/or retain our forgiveness. In the teachings of Christ, we learn that unless we forgive, God will not forgive us. In the Lord's Prayer says, "And forgive us our debts, *as we forgive our debtors. . .*" (Matthew 6:12). He continues: "For if you forgive men their trespasses, your heavenly Father will also forgive you. *But if you do not forgive men their trespasses, neither will your Father forgive your trespasses*" (Matthew 6:14-15).

A forgiven person must love much and must show forth the power of Him who has forgiven them. Christ says in Luke 7: 47 (to a "sinner" who anointed Him with a precious ointment), "her sins, which are many, are forgiven, for she loved much. But to whom little is forgiven, the same loves little. . . ."

Simply put, the woman had enormous love for Christ as a result of His forgiveness. It changed her life. This is related to 1 John 4: 19, "We love Him because he first loved us." This 'first love' is the death of Christ as the only basis of God's ability to forgive us. When the sinner realizes this, his heart is broken and he loves in return, to the extent of giving his life to the One who forgave him.

When we refuse to forgive as Christ forgave, we deprive people of exposure to the power that can change them! This is why we will not receive or retain our forgiveness.

Our unforgiving spirit tests our love and loyalty to God. The story of Job teaches that our severe trials—including the hurts and tragedies we have suffered—reveal whether or not we love God. When Satan asked, "Does Job fear God for nothing?" (Job 1:9), he was, in effect, saying that Christians cannot continue serving the Lord when they suffer major hurts. Or as he put it, "Skin for skin! Yes, all that a man has he will give for his life. But stretch out Your hand now, and touch his bone and his flesh, and he will surely curse You to Your face!" (Job 2:3-5).

In the great controversy between Christ and Satan, our response to hurts is a vote for or against God. We either glorify God or betray and mock Him by our attitude to adversities inflicted upon us by others. Whether or not we forgive and forget reveals our true love or loyalty to God.

You see, the fundamental issue at stake whenever we face any trials (including hurts and losses) are these: will we continue to trust God, believing that He knows what is best for us, and that He has *power* to sustain and deliver us? Will we do what He has asked us (in this case, forgive others) even in cases of illness, financial crises, embarrassment, pain, disappointment, ridicule, rejection, and death (cf. Job 19:6-27)? Or will we only do His will when things go our way?

Perhaps you have been hurt by someone near or dear—perhaps a relative, co-worker, husband, or wife. The one who has seriously wounded you could even be in the church. You may have been hurt, betrayed, defrauded, humiliated, violated, or wounded by a church member, elder, Sabbath school teacher, or pastor. And you cannot bring yourself to forgive. Perhaps you are still hurt and angry.

It could be that, even right now, as you read this page, your marriage is falling apart. Perhaps you are considering an unbiblical divorce (cf. Matthew 19:9) because of the hurt and pain you have suffered in your marriage. If so, I'd urge you to reconsider your decision and prayerfully explore the path of forgiveness and reconciliation.

Regardless of the cause of your hurt, remember that your hurt is part of the great controversy between Christ and Satan. And in the light of that cosmic conflict, the Lord urges you to make a conscious decision to forgive the perpetrator of that crime. For as long as you still carry the bitterness and resentment, you will never be free. You will forever remain a slave of the person who has hurt you.

While we may not always understand why people choose to hurt us, the Lord can bring something good out of our painful experiences—if we make a decision to forgive. The story of Joseph illustrates this point. After experiencing all sorts of injustice—jealousy, malice, and hatred from his brothers, harassment, blackmail, and false accusation from Mrs. Portiphar, the injustice of imprisonment in an Egyptian jail, and being forgotten by one of the prisoners—the Bible records that Joseph later understands that even in the midst of his terrible ordeal, God's divine hands were still directing affairs for his good and the good of humanity.

His forgiving spirit is evident in the following enduring words he spoke to his brothers: "But now, do not therefore be grieved or angry with yourselves because you sold me here; *for God sent me before you to preserve life* . . . But as for you, you meant evil against me; *but God meant it for good,* in order to bring it about as it is this day, to save many people alive (Genesis 45:5; 50:20).

So writes Ellen G. White:

> He who is imbued with the Spirit of Christ abides in Christ. Whatever comes to him comes from the Saviour, who surrounds him with His presence. Nothing can touch him except by the Lord's permission. All our sufferings and sorrows, all our temptations and trials, all our sadness and griefs, all our persecutions and privations, in short, all things work together for our good. All experiences and circumstances are God's workmen whereby good is brought to us (*Ministry of Healing,* 489).

Perhaps a fitting way to conclude is to look briefly at how David treated Saul, a man who sought to kill David on several occasions.

David and Saul

Our discussion of David and Mephibosheth began with a frantic question from King David: ""Is there still anyone who is *left of the house of Saul,* that I may show him kindness for Jonathan's sake?" (2 Samuel 9:1). Observe that David was not simply interested in Mephibosheth (whose existence he did not even know), but rather in "the house of Saul"—the house of his worse enemy.

The relationship between David and Saul is captured in the book of First Samuel. Saul hated David, and he tried to kill David on several occasions—for no other reason than pure jealousy. David had been anointed as king in place of Saul when the latter was rejected by God. And the women sang the praises of David when he killed Goliath—a feat that Saul couldn't do. All these contributed to Saul's jealousy and hatred, and his psychopathic desire to kill David.

In contrast, whenever David had the opportunity to kill his archenemy Saul, he always chose to spare his life. He constantly displayed magnanimity towards his worse foe. This fact is best illustrated in one incident recorded in 1 Samuel 26. At the time of this story, Saul, together with some 3,000 soldiers were pursuing David. It was evident that Saul would stop at nothing to murder the youthful David. Earlier, he had murdered eighty-five innocent priests and their families, in cold blood because they helped David and his men.

In the incident we're about to review, David, along with his security man Abishai, slipped into Saul's camp, into the very tent that Saul was sleeping. None of Saul's men saw David and his associate because God had put Saul and all his soldiers in a deep sleep. When Abishai saw David's archenemy sleeping, he whispered into his ears the need for swift justice: "Today God has delivered your enemy into your hands. Now let me pin him to the ground with one thrust of my spear; I won't strike him twice" (1 Samuel 26:8; NIV).

David had very good reasons why he could have killed Saul. First, Saul and his 3,000 soldiers were out to kill David and his followers. Here was a perfect opportunity to kill an enemy in self-defense. It was a perfect case of pre-emptive strike. Moreover, God—through Samuel—had anointed David as the next king of Israel. Furthermore, God had put Saul's entire army into a deep sleep so that David and Abishai could walk right up to Saul. Why else would God do this?

Though David had some legitimate justification and opportunity to mortally wound his enemy, David chose not to do so.

> But David said to Abishai, "Don't destroy him! Who can lay a hand on the LORD's anointed and be guiltless? As surely as the LORD lives," he said, "the LORD himself will strike him; either his time will come and he will die, or he will go into battle and perish. But the LORD forbid that I should lay a hand on the LORD's anointed. Now get the spear and water jug that are near his head, and let's go" (1 Samuel 26:8-11; NIV).

David offered forgiveness to his mortal enemy, trusting his case with God Himself. What is even more remarkable is how David reacted when some time later, Saul and his sons were killed in a battle with the Philistines.

David could have said, "Saul got what he deserved!" But he didn't. Instead of rejoicing at the death of his enemy, David even composed a song for the people of Judah to sing in honor of Saul and his sons. He strongly urged the people not to proclaim the death in the streets of the Philistine cities lest the enemy rejoice. David also decreed that there should be no rain or crops in the place where Saul was slain, suggesting that he wanted to mark that spot for remembrance. Finally David called for all of Israel to weep over Saul (2 Samuel 1:17-27).

The spirit of David was a forgiving and magnanimous spirit. Not only did he freely forgive the one who constantly sought his destruction, he also did not rejoice at the misfortune of his enemy. David was deeply pained when his archrival Saul was hurt.

The heart of David reveals the heart of God. For our heavenly Father showers his blessings upon both the good and the evil. Thus, on the Sermon on the Mount Jesus urges his followers to show forgiveness even to our enemies:

You have heard that it was said, 'Love your neighbor and hate your enemy.' But I tell you: Love your enemies and pray for those who persecute you, that you may be sons of your Father in heaven. He causes his sun to rise on the evil and the good, and sends rain on the righteous and the unrighteous (Matthew 5:43-45).

But I tell you who hear me: Love your enemies, do good to those who hate you, bless those who curse you, pray for those who mistreat you. If someone strikes you on one cheek, turn to him the other also. If someone takes your cloak, do not stop him from taking your tunic. Give to everyone who asks you, and if anyone takes what belongs to you, do not demand it back. Do to others as you would have them do to you. If you love those who love you, what credit is that to you? Even 'sinners' love those who love them. And if you do good to those who are good to you, what credit is that to you? Even 'sinners' do that. And if you lend to those from whom you expect repayment, what credit is that to you? Even 'sinners' lend to 'sinners,' expecting to be repaid in full. But love your enemies, do good to them, and lend to them without expecting to get anything back. Then your reward will be great, and you will be sons of the Most High, because he is kind to the ungrateful and wicked. Be merciful, just as your Father is merciful (Luke 6:27-36).

Conclusion

If you are struggling with unforgiveness, remind yourself of how God has forgiven you and respond in kind:

The LORD is merciful and gracious,
    Slow to anger, and abounding in mercy.
He will not always strive with us,
    Nor will He keep His anger forever.
He has not dealt with us according to our sins,
    Nor punished us according to our iniquities.

For as the heavens are high above the earth,
So great is His mercy toward those who fear Him;
As far as the east is from the west,
So far has He removed our transgressions from us (Psalm 103:8-12).

Forgiveness is possible when you understand and have experienced God's own forgiveness. Refusal to forgive as Christ has forgiven us is an indication that we have not truly experienced the life-changing work of God's forgiveness.

You may not have had a choice over the actions of the people who inflicted painful wounds upon you. But you do have a choice over how you respond to those who have hurt you. You can choose to forgive them. An unwillingness to forgive suggests that you yourself have not been truly healed.

It is true that you are hurting from the wounds that others inflicted upon you. But as I stated at the beginning of this chapter, as painful as your wounds may be, there is another wound which is worse than those that have been inflicted upon you by others. *The worst wounds that can ever be inflicted upon you are those you inflict upon yourself by your decision not to forgive your wound-ers.* The sin of unforgiveness can be fatal to the quality of your life now and can affect your eternal destiny.

Now is the time to let go—to forgive—the people who have hurt you.

Are your scars still bleeding? Are you still wondering why you must forgive and forget? The story of David and Mephibosheth teaches that the most compelling reason to forgive is not because that individual deserves it or because the person has asked for it, but for Jonathan's sake. Forgiveness "for Christ's sake" is the healing balm for our suicidal wounds.

Endnotes

1. Luke 7:42-43; 2 Corinthians 2:7-10; Ephesians 4:32; Colossians 3:13.
2. Cf. Isaiah 53:4-6; 1 Peter 1:24-25.

Chapter 12
SCARS OF LOVE

We all carry scars. Some scars are very small and don't really matter. Others are big and evoke memories—recollections of past accidents and mistakes or of some deeply distressing experiences. I'm not simply referring to scars left on our bodies. I have in mind scars left on our souls—the consequences of some past decisions or actions. The ugly scars of sin.

Scars are signs of pain and healing. They mark spots where we once received fresh wounds. They remind us that although healing has taken place, the spot we received the wound will never be the same again.

Behind every scar is a story. Some are humorous. Others are tragic and sad. Some of us have more scars than others. If the wounds that left behind the scars were very deep or big, the scars tend to be more prominent—causing embarrassment, shame, or emotional pain. In some cases our scars are so ugly that we try to hide them from curious eyes.

Incredible as it may seem, not all ugly scars are bad. Sometimes our ugly scars are good! For they remind us of our major deliverance—of worse situations that could have happened, but didn't, when we received the wounds.

I don't know the source of the following story that was shared with me several years ago. But it aptly illustrates what I call "good ugly scars."

Good Ugly Scars

Some years ago on a hot summer day in south Florida, a little boy decided to go for a swim in the old swimming hole behind his house. In a hurry to dive into the cool water, he ran out the back door, leaving behind shoes, socks, and shirt as he went. He flew into the water, not realizing that as he swam toward the middle of the lake, an alligator was swimming toward the shore. His mother in the house was looking out the window and saw the two as they got closer and closer together. In utter fear, she ran toward the water, yelling to her son as loudly as she could.

Hearing her voice, the little boy became alarmed and made a U-turn to swim to his mother. It was too late. Just as he reached her, the alligator reached him. From the dock, the mother grabbed her little boy by the arms just as the alligator snatched his legs. That began an incredible tug-of-war between the two. The alligator was much stronger than the mother, but the mother was much too passionate to let go.

A farmer happened to drive by, heard her screams, raced from his truck, took aim and shot the alligator. Remarkably, after weeks and weeks in the hospital, the little boy survived. His legs were extremely scarred by the vicious attack of the animal. And on his arms were deep scratches where his mother's fingernails dug into his flesh in her effort to hang on to the son she loved.

A newspaper reporter who interviewed the boy after the trauma asked if he would show him his scars. The boy lifted his pant legs. And then, with obvious pride, he said to the reporter, "But look at my arms. *I have great scars on my arms, too. I have them because my Mom wouldn't let go.*"

You and I can identify with that little boy. We, too, have scars. No, not scars from an alligator, but scars of a painful past. The scars of wrong choices that have caused us deep regret. The scars that resulted when we thoughtlessly waded into dangerous situations, not knowing what lay ahead.

The good news, however, is that for every wound that has been healed, there are also some other kinds of scars. I call them "scars of love." They are scars that have been left behind because, like the mom of that little boy, God has refused to let go. In the midst of our struggle, He's been there holding on to us. He's been holding on to us through the pains of trials and afflictions. He's been holding on through the discipline and corrections of life.

The scars of love are also scars of warning. Each time we see those scars, we are reminded that we should not go back to the places of peril we once were delivered from. Furthermore, because of our scars, others may be warned against repeating our mistakes.

The swimming hole of life is filled with peril—and we often forget that the enemy is waiting to attack. That's when the tug-of-war begins. Through our wrong choices, the enemy inflicts some ugly scars on our souls.

But, oh, there are also some other scars—scars left behind by a loving Father who did not—and will never—let us go. The reason He didn't let go is because His own Son received an ugly scar to rescue us. The Word of God says this of Christ Jesus:

> He was wounded for our transgressions,
> He was bruised for our iniquities;
> The chastisement of our peace was upon Him,
> And by His stripes we are healed (Isaiah 53:5).

In the chapter on "Calvary," the author of *The Desire of Ages* describes the day Christ was wounded in the following words:

> The spotless Son of God hung upon the cross, His flesh lacerated with stripes; those hands so often reached out in blessing, nailed to the wooden bars; those feet so tireless on ministries of love, spiked to the tree; that royal head pierced by the crown of thorns; those quivering lips shaped to the cry of woe. And all that He endured—the blood drops that flowed from His head, His hands, His feet, the agony that racked His frame, and the unutterable anguish that filled His soul at the hiding of His Father's face—speaks to each child of humanity, declaring, It is for thee that the Son of God consents to bear this burden of guilt; for thee He spoils the domain of death, and opens the gates of Paradise. He who stilled the angry waves and walked the foam-capped billows, who made devils tremble and disease flee, who opened blind eyes and called forth the dead to life, —offers Himself upon the cross as a sacrifice, and this from love to thee. He, the Sin Bearer, endures the wrath of divine justice, and for thy sake becomes sin itself.[1]

On Calvary's cross, "He was *wounded* for our transgressions, He was *bruised* for our iniquities . . . And by His stripes *we are healed.*" Yes, in the scars of Christ we can today find healing for our own ugly scars. Praise the Lord—"by His stripes we are healed"!

Scars of Hope

Yes, our Lord Jesus Christ Himself bears some scars: in His hands, side, and feet. His scars are reminders of wounds inflicted upon Him when He came to die for us. But in the scars of Christ, all who carry ugly scars can find healing and hope.

On that Good Friday—the day of His crucifixion—evil men drove nails into His hands and feet, and they thrust a spear into His side. When He rose triumphantly from the dead on Easter Sunday, His glorious body still bore the scars of His past suffering, pain, and death. But instead of hiding those scars because of shame, Christ displays them to give us comfort, assurance, and hope.

The Gospel of John tells us that on the resurrection day Our Lord Jesus Christ invited doubting Thomas to behold His scars so he might know He was real and believe:

> On the evening of that first day of the week, when the disciples were together, with the doors locked for fear of the Jews, Jesus came and stood among them and said, "Peace be with you!" After he said this, he showed them his hands and side. The disciples were overjoyed when they saw the Lord. Again Jesus said, "Peace be with you! As the Father has sent me, I am sending you." And with that he breathed on them and said, "Receive the Holy Spirit. If you forgive anyone his sins, they are forgiven; if you do not forgive them, they are not forgiven." Now Thomas (called Didymus), one of the Twelve, was not with the disciples when Jesus came. So the other disciples told him, "We have seen the Lord!" But he said to them, "Unless I see the nail marks in his hands and put my finger where the nails were, and put my hand into his side, I will not believe it." A week later his disciples were in the house again, and Thomas was with them. Though the doors were locked, Jesus came and stood among them and said, "Peace be with you!" Then he said to Thomas, "Put your finger here; see my hands. Reach out your hand and put it into my side. Stop doubting and believe." Thomas said to him, "My Lord and my God!" Then Jesus told him, "Because you

> have seen me, you have believed; blessed are those who have not seen and yet have believed." (John 20:19-29; NIV)

Yes, our risen Savior also carries scars—some ugly scars in His hands, feet, and side. He did not hide His scars. But rather, through the scars He identified with the disappointment, fears, doubts, and pain of Thomas—and every other follower of Christ.

In the scars of Christ, every human scar can find healing.

But there's more. Even when we get to heaven, the scars of Christ will be an eternal reminder of what He did to save us. We turn now to the words of the Old Testament prophet Zechariah to describe what will happen one day when we also see our loving Saviour:

> "And one shall say unto him, What are these wounds in thine hands? Then he shall answer, Those with which I was wounded in the house of my friends" (Zechariah 13:6 KJV).[2]

From Calvary to all eternity, we discover why our Lord would not let go of us. The print of the nails—the scars of Christ—will tell the story of our wonderful redemption and the dear price by which it was purchased. The scars of love will become the scars of our eternal certainty.

If we have repented of our sins and accepted Christ as our Savior and Lord, then we need not continue suffering shame, guilt, and pain from our ugly scars. In the scars of Christ, we find hope and healing for all our ugly scars. Therefore, in the words of Isaac Watts, let us go back to Calvary and "survey the wondrous cross on which the Prince of Glory died." Let us "See from His head, His hands, His feet" and ask why He suffered so much. When we do so, His scars will transform our own ugly scars of pain and regret into scars of hope.

When I survey the wondrous cross
On which the Prince of glory died,
My richest gain I count but loss,
And pour contempt on all my pride.

Forbid it, Lord, that I should boast,
Save in the death of Christ my God!
All the vain things that charm me most,
I sacrifice them to His blood.

See from His head, His hands, His feet,
Sorrow and love flow mingled down!
Did e'er such love and sorrow meet,
Or thorns compose so rich a crown?

His dying crimson, like a robe,
Spreads o'er His body on the tree;
Then I am dead to all the globe,
And all the globe is dead to me.

Were the whole realm of nature mine,
That were a present far too small;
Love so amazing, so divine,
Demands my soul, my life, my all.

[Added by the compilers of Hymns Ancient and Modern]

To Christ, Who won for sinners grace
By bitter grief and anguish sore,
Be praise from all the ransomed race
Forever and forevermore.

Endnotes

1. E. G. White, *The Desire of Ages,* pp. 755-756

2. Some Bible scholars and interpreters have applied this text to Christ as predictive of His scourging and wounds received at the hands of those who should have been His friends (see Matt. 27:26; Mark 14:65; 15:15; Luke 22:63; John 19:1, 17, 18). This must be done by secondary application or by making a break after Zechariah 13:5 and by connecting v. 6 with v. 7, which is clearly predictive of Christ (Matt. 26:31).

Chapter 13
MEDITATIONS ON SCARS OF LOVE

True Christian meditation, in contrast to other forms of meditation, is an active thought process, in which the believer seeks to fill his or her mind with truths about God. It is not the emptying of one's mind. Rather, it is thinking or reflecting on God's Word, praying and asking God to give us understanding by the Spirit, who has promised to lead us "into all truth" (John 16:13).

The product of Christian meditation must always be in harmony with the teachings of God's Word. It must also lead to an authentic Christian spirituality, lifestyle, and an adoration, praise, and service for Christ.

One of the biblical themes we can profitably meditate upon is the life of Christ. For in Christ, we live, and move, and have our being (Acts 17:28). Thus, we read from the pen of the now familiar Christian devotional writer of the nineteenth-century:

> It would be well to spend a thoughtful hour each day reviewing the life of Christ from the manger to Calvary. We should take it point by point, and let the imagination vividly grasp each scene, especially the closing ones of his earthly life. By thus contemplating his teachings and sufferings, and the infinite sacrifice made by him for the redemption of the race, we may strengthen our faith, quicken our love, and become more deeply imbued with the spirit which sustained our Saviour. If we would be saved at last, we must learn the lesson of penitence and faith at the foot of the cross. . . . Everything noble and generous in man will respond to the contemplation of Christ upon the cross.[1]

This chapter consists of the reflections by some public university students on the wounds and scars of Christ. These students—the current CAMPUS missionaries and five Indiana University students who had joined the missionaries during their Spring Break—were given the opportunity to read sections of this book's draft manuscript and to share their thoughts on the previous chapter—the "Scars of Love."[2]

A Balm for our Wounds

Dora Boateng
Graduate of Case Western Reserve University, Ohio (Psychology & Pre-Med);
CAMPUS Missionary

The joy in knowing that there is healing in Christ is very comforting. Unfortunately, it is often the case that we are too engrossed in our pain to seek healing from our Lord. The Prophet Jeremiah (8:22) asks the question "Is there no balm in Gilead? Is there no healing there? Why then is the health of the daughter of my people not restored?"

When wounds are bleeding and they are still fresh, this is the time when Christ is closest to us. Our Savior is always ready to grant us healing and remove from us the hurt and pain. He bids us: "Come to me, all ye that labor and are heavy laden . . . and ye shall find rest unto your souls" (Matthew 11:28-29).

There is good news in knowing that God has already provided us with healing; it is amazing that before we were wounded, He had the balm ready! He sent His son Jesus Christ to die for us and, "with His stripes, we are healed" (Isaiah 53:5). Furthermore, the Bible says in Revelation 21:4 that when we get to heaven, "God shall wipe away all tears from our eyes, and there shall be no more death, nor sorrow, nor pain . . . for the former things are passed away." Not only can we look to God for healing, but we can also look forward to having our scars removed permanently when we get to heaven.

Regardless of our pain and suffering, Christ is ever ready to relieve us of our aching and bleeding wounds. Give your pain and hurt to Jesus; He will provide the balm to soothe and calm your soul.

The Evidence of Love

Carl E. Brugger
Student, Indiana University (Computer Science)

Scars are often things we want to hide from the public. They are reminders of pain and hurt. However, there are some scars that we can take pride in. We can take pride in the scars left in a Savior who fought to save us from the pain and suffering of this world. Through His suffering, He has provided a way for us to be healed.

One of my favorite quotes is from *The Desire of Ages* page 25. E. G. White writes:

> Christ was treated as we deserve, that we might be treated as He deserves. He was condemned for our sins, in which He had no share, that we might be justified by His righteousness, in which we had no share. He suffered the death which was ours, that we might receive the life which was His. "With His stripes we are healed."

I am continually amazed in the fact that Christ suffered so much for a race of sinful human beings. His suffering has become a way for each of us to be healed from the pain and hurt caused by sin. By showing us His scars, He is reminding us that there is still hope, that He is fighting for our salvation. It reminds me of the verse in John 15:13: "Greater love hath no man than this, that a man lay down his life for his friends." Jesus truly showed that love towards us!

Scars Are Unfeeling

Jonathan Martin
Graduate of Sierra College California (Pre-Med);
CAMPUS Missionary

Scars are unfeeling. Depending on what caused the injury, thick layers of skin may develop and cause that region to be numb to a normal touch. Something is felt, but the sensation is dulled; the full force is not felt.

In many ways, my response to the story of Jesus' death is like that. I've heard it before; the freshness is gone. A full-frontal attack with the story, a dry rehearsal of the facts, may produce a dulled response or an intellectual assent. But there must be more.

As I muse on this hardness of heart, I'm reminded of Thomas' story. He, too, could not be reached by a rehearsal of the facts. It was a personal, unexpected encounter with the risen Jesus that made the difference, that navigated around his callused spot, and thrilled his soul with the reality of a crucified and risen Savior.

It is the unexpected events that reach past my callused spots: stepping outside and looking up to see a spectacular cloudburst or reflecting on a Bible story while walking on the treadmill. Each is an experience that started ordinarily but ended with a fresh glimpse of God.

Jesus is still in the business of reaching past unfeeling hearts and of creating unexpected encounters. It's a commitment as lasting as the scars He bears.

Scars for Our Salvation

Daniel Goodin
Graduate of Indiana University (Mathematics);
AmeriCorps Math Matters Tutor Coordinator

When I consider how most scars come about, they seem to be the result of unwise choices. The scars might be from a fight, or from trying to pet a strange dog, or from some other instance that could have been avoided. But in the story of the boy and the alligator, the scars on the boy's arms were the result of his mother's unwillingness to let go of him and give him up to die. Those scars were the result of unyielding love. The harm she inflicted on her son prevented the alligator from claiming his prize.

Likewise, although we may not initially see them for what they are, some of the scars that have been inflicted upon us, both physically and emotionally, are certainly scars of love. They are God's efforts to save us from destruction and pull us back to Him. Yet the greatest examples of scars of love are those that are on our Savior.

Our scars can eventually be healed, but His will remain. Every time that boy looks at his arms, he will be reminded of his mother's unyielding love. Every time we see Christ's scars, we will be reminded of His unyielding love for us through His sacrifice. Those are truly scars of love.

Too Deep for Words

David Park
Student, University of Maryland (Electrical Engineering);
CAMPUS Missionary

Love is so deep, so encompassing, so powerful, that it cannot be merely expressed with words. It isn't simply information, conveying an idea or a thought. By nature, love is shown and understood demonstratively. So when a man loves a woman, it is not enough to verbally express his love for her, even if he has done it a thousand times. Why? Because the woman wants to see for herself that he loves her. She will say "show me."

In the same way, the accusation that was laid against God at the beginning of the Great Controversy was that He really didn't love His children. So what did God do? If we examine John 3:16 it says, "For God so loved the world, that He gave His only begotten Son, that whoever believes in Him shall not perish, but have eternal life" (NASB). The problem was that, due to sin, humanity was lost! And in order for God to express that He still loved His people and did not in fact want them to perish, He had to show the universe. The verse doesn't say, "For God so loved the world, that He said it was so." It says that He gave His only begotten Son to pay the price of sin. He went to that great of a length to demonstrate His love. The whole universe—including the heavenly host at Calvary—saw at that moment when Jesus died, that God was indeed love.

When we as Christians attend church, or spiritual gatherings, not a single person will ever say "No," when asked if he or she loves Jesus. But Christ is looking at our hearts and asking us, just as He asked Peter, "Do you love Me?" And then, He says to us, "Show Me." It is not good enough for us to say mere words to express love. Words wouldn't do justice, wouldn't satisfy, and wouldn't be sufficient for such a profound concept. Our purpose in life is to reflect God's character.

If Christ went to an infinite length to show His love for us, then the questions we Christians need to constantly ask ourselves are these: "How can I show my love back?"; "In what ways can I show more love to my Savior?"; and "Is what I'm doing now, demonstrating my love for Him?"

Christ has shown us His love, and He has permanent scars to prove it: scars that are too deep for words.

Undefinable Love

Brennen Varneck
Rock-Climbing Instructor, Alberta, Canada;
CAMPUS Missionary

"And one shall say unto him, What are these wounds in thine hands? Then he shall answer, Those with which I was wounded in the house of my friends" (Zechariah 13:6, KJV).

Zechariah 13:6 is such a new thought for me—assuming this Old Testament passage can legitimately be applied to Christ. First of all, why would someone have to even ask "what are these wounds in thine hands?" Do they not know? Yes, many will be in the kingdom and not even know who Jesus is. They accepted the Holy Spirit's promptings to live selflessly and have received the gift of eternal life. But just imagine their own shock when Jesus says that He received the wounds "in the house of my friends."

"YOUR FRIENDS! You got those (pointing at the scars) at your friends' place?" is what you can hear them saying. With a smile on His face, Jesus nods. As the inquiry is being made about the scars, one of the redeemed who took part in giving those very wounds overhears the conversation and begins to weep. He weeps because he can remember Jesus praying out of love for him saying, "Father please forgive them, for they know not what they do." He weeps out of joy and the sheer love exuberating out of Christ.

Romans 5:10 says "For if, when we were enemies, we were reconciled to God by the death of His Son, much more, being reconciled, we shall be saved by His life." Jesus' love is so great that He calls us who were once an enemy, His friends. I cannot simply wrap my mind around such an idea. I praise His name that it is not just an idea but the truth of the whole gospel.

When I see such truth I begin to understand Jeremiah 31:3: "I have loved thee with an everlasting love; therefore, with loving kindness have I drawn thee." How God draws us to Himself! Jesus, I give you my all, and I lay my life down. Reader, I appeal to you; will you do the same in the glorious face of infinite love?

Scars of Love

Christine Brugger

Student, Indiana University (Mathematics)

Since the time that sin entered the world, all of humanity has been wounded and bears the scars of its sinful nature. This is illustrated by the story of the little boy who was attacked by the alligator. In this story, there were two types of scars mentioned.

The first were the ones left by the alligator. These represent the scars that sin leaves in our lives. Every time we sin, even if we repent and ask forgiveness, we are left with a mark from that sin that won't disappear.

The second type of scars mentioned were the scars from his mother holding on so tightly. I believe that this is representative of God's unending efforts to rescue us from the snares of sin. This reminds me of something I heard in a sermon recently. Sometimes God, in His infinite love for us, has to allow us to suffer in order for us to realize our deep need for Him. He lets us endure the consequences of our actions. He does not wish to cause us pain, but it is only through seeing the pain and suffering caused by a sinful world that we will have that deep desire and longing for Him.

Once we have realized that this world has nothing to offer us, and we decide to fully consecrate ourselves to God, He can start His work of healing. But those scars will still remain to remind us of the ugliness of sin and the suffering that it inflicts on those who yield to it. Only after Jesus' second coming and the abolition of sin, will all of these scars be removed from us. "And God shall wipe away all tears from their eyes; and there shall be no more death, neither sorrow, nor crying, neither shall there be any more pain: for the former things are passed away" (Revelation 21:4). The only reminder of the painfulness and destructive nature of sin will be the scars in Jesus' hands, feet, and side. These will remain throughout eternity to remind us of the consequences of sin.

Scars of Jesus

Abigail Koo
Currently pursuing Doctor of Music degree in Instrumental Conducting at Indiana University

Our Heavenly Father is more than able to remove all scars. He promised us that He will wipe away all tears, and there will be no more sorrow in His Kingdom (Revelation 21:4). At His second coming, in a twinkling of an eye, our bodies will be translated into immortality. I will no longer have the big birthmark on my left shoulder, and all scars left from bruises and stitches will be removed. I will have a clean body like a newborn baby.

However, when Jesus was resurrected, His body bore scars from the cross; He will have them forever. Why, God? Why can't Jesus have a clean body, as we will inherit? Why does Jesus have to bear those awful scars forever? The consequence of my sin is that great. Its results are eternal, and Jesus took them all. The shame, guilt, pain, scars, death . . . True love causes one to bear another's consequences despite its ugliness, pain, and permanence.

Justice and mercy: when I want to make things "right", it's at the expense of mercy, and vice versa; show mercy at the expense of justice. To have both justice and mercy costs my wants, my needs, my feelings . . . and that is very difficult for my selfish nature.

Our Creator loved mercy that before we even sinned; He knew that He was going to forgive us. Our Creator is just, so He had to let sin take its course.

He reconciled both justice and mercy at the expense of Himself.

My Jesus bears my scars and He will have them forever.

He allows me to have scars in my life now, physical and emotional, that I may remember the ugliness of sin but, more importantly, the mercy of Jesus who bore it all for me.

For us this is temporary; for Him, it will be forever.

That's unfair, isn't it?

That's grace: the unfair gift of love.

Scars of Devotion

Kayla Pina
Graduate of Harvard University, Massachusetts (Sociology);
CAMPUS Missionary

Jesus hung on that cross for six hours. The weight of His body must have deepened the pain of the nails driven through His hands and feet. It must have caused the flesh to separate more with time, creating not just a hole, but a gaping hole. And these marks He has chosen to keep for eternity. When He returns, every saved soul shall be changed in the twinkling of an eye, and our corrupt, tired, deteriorated bodies will be made incorruptible (1 Corinthians 15:51-51). God will wipe all tears from our eyes (Revelation 21:4). As we repent, He throws our sins into the depths of the sea (Micah 7:19).

But the marks that represent Jesus' death for our sins will remain forever. Jesus' wounds are the only ones that bring healing—"with His stripes we are healed"—but His will never disappear.

Jesus was wounded in His hands, feet, head, and side. The only wound that will remain hidden behind His kingly robes of righteousness is the one wound He received once He could no longer feel the blow. The wounds He received in His head, hands, and feet, that He received while He was still able to feel pain, are the readily visible wounds, the ones forever visible to those who look upon the Redeemer of the world.

Yet Jesus' greatest suffering was not in the physical aspect, but in the spiritual: sin had caused separation between God and His creation, and it broke Jesus' heart. He was willing to be wounded for the sake of others' salvation, that we might be reconciled to God. He despised pain and shame for the sake of humanity and willingly bore marks that for anyone else would be marks of ignominy. Every time the Father, Son, and Holy Ghost see those marks, they "shall see of the travail of his soul, and shall be satisfied" (Isaiah 53:11).

Can I have the same degree of devotion to the cause of God?

In seeking to be like my Lord, I want to be able to say, like Paul, that I am "always bearing about in the body the dying of the Lord Jesus...that the life also of Jesus might be made manifest in [my] mortal flesh" (2 Corinthians 4:10, 11). As I have this experience, in being willing to bear scars of love for the sake of others' salvation, I hope that when I meet my dear Savior face-to-face, I'll better appreciate the pain He bore and witness for myself the sacrifice He made that I may be with Him.

The Scars of God

By Verleen K. McSween
Currently pursuing a PhD in Vision Science, Indiana University

Christ's scars serve as evidence and a testimony of the Love of God for mankind. His scars of pain, embarrassment, scorn, humiliation, suffering, persecution, and mortal death reveal much about the character of God. Wounds once fresh have been healed. Yet scars remain as a testimony. Though Christ was inflicted with wounds as a result of sin, He will shamelessly and humbly bear them throughout eternity. Yet He offers sinful man, who ought to bear those scars, a glorified body. I imagine this body to be a perfect form, no longer vulnerable to mortal wounds, nor bounded by sin's reward . . . death. No remnants of the painful things of the past will remain; for this reason, I smile.

Now, when I look at my body and see my earthly scars, I am disgusted. They are unsightly and resurrect memories and emotions once laid to rest. My scars serve as a living diary, whose pages are made of flesh. What about Christ? What about His scars? Wasn't it I who wounded my God and left these scars? When I will look upon my Savior throughout eternity—time with no end—I will never forget, deny, or doubt His Love. Why? Those scars, His scars will be an emblem of something so beautiful that it cannot be expressed by human tongue. It can only be expressed by the language of heaven, which we mortals have yet to learn. I suppose it has been translated into a form we can easily understand—the scars of God.

We know that the Law of God is a manifestation of His character. The Law reflects His authority, His justice, and His righteousness. But the scars of God are also a manifestation of His character. These scars reflect His mercy, His compassion, and His humility. They will be my

God's testimony to an entire universe and all created beings of His immense desire to humble Himself for the restoration of men to the family of God. If you don't believe me, I'll let you hear it from His own mouth. He declares, "Wherefore thou art no more a servant, but a son, and if a son, then an heir of God through Christ" (Galatians 4:7). How lovely are the scars of God!

Power in the Scars

Cassandra Papenfuse
Graduate of University of Michgian (African Studies and International Health); CAMPUS Missionary

God never promised a life free from pain and ugly scars, even for his followers. Christ promised his disciples that pain, trials, and persecutions would come (Mark 10:29-30). While we live on this earth and in this fallen world, we will always be surrounded with wickedness that hurts us and leaves scars. But there is a purpose for scars.

If we never had pain or scars we would never understand the ugliness of sin and the extent to which it really destroys and hurts. After the fall in the garden, Adam and Eve's first encounter with the repercussions of sin, pain and death, was when God killed an animal to clothe them (Genesis 3:21). God wanted them to see the contrast between his character, kingdom and perfect laws, and sin. The more we come into communion with God and discover the brightness of His glory, and are changed into that glory (2 Corinthians 3:18), we realize we were not made for this world. We were not created to live in a place that causes pain and hurt—that leaves scars.

That's why the concept that Christ partook in the scars of this earthly world so that we may enter a heavenly world clean and free, with unblemished, glorified bodies is purely amazing. He took on scars out of love for humanity, for His creation. Though it wasn't God's plan for us to understand or partake in sin, to receive scars from our actions or the actions of others, He made a counter plan to free His children from bondage. Part of that plan had to include scars and bruising.

When we survey the cross, we realize that there is no power in scars unless we take on the scars of Christ and allow ourselves to be crucified with Him (Matthew 16:24). When we are crucified with Christ, God can use our scars to minister to others. We can show the scars from our fallen past, and then the scars from crucifixion, and proclaim, "How great is it to bear these scars of love!" God can use our scars to point others with similar scars to the cross. But it isn't until we can testify of Christ and the love that He has shown, that God can use those scars. Am I allowing God to use my scars?

Recognizing Our Scars

Michel Lee
Student, Stanford University (Pre-Med);
CAMPUS Missionary

The crux of understanding Christ's scars of love is not so much whether we carry scars or not. It is recognizing that we have scars. It is only when we recognize our pitiful condition as sinful man that Christ's redeeming sacrifice can take full effect in our lives.

One of the characteristics of the last-day church is a failure to recognize our need of Christ. John the Revelator describes the church of the Laodiceans as such: "Because thou [the Laodiceans] sayest, I am rich, and increased with goods, and have need of nothing; and knowest not that thou art wretched, and miserable, and poor, and blind, and naked" (Revelation 4:17). Examine your innermost intentions, your struggles, your temptations—yes, we really are wretched, miserable, poor, blind, and naked! Think of the times that you have failed yourself and others. We must rest instead on the unfailing merits of Christ.

But come to think of it, recognizing scars and our consequent need for a Savior has been man's perpetual struggle since the beginning of time, even before human scars existed. Because Eve did not depend on God's provision for her, and preferred to "be as gods," she took of the forbidden fruit, and by similar reasoning, so did Adam (Genesis 3:5). Lack of dependence on God is not a trifling matter—it was sin—and it immediately necessitated Christ's wounds.

Living now in a world pervaded by sin, we have been offered Christ's scars in exchange for our own. Romans 3:23 reads, "For all have sinned, and come short of the glory of God." Yet repentance and recognition of our state comes only from the Holy Spirit—we must plead for this gift!—by the study of God's Word. "[B]y the law is the knowledge of sin," writes Paul (Romans 3:20). Behold Christ and His matchless charms, His incomprehensible sacrifice, and we cannot help but plead for Him to cover us with His blood.

Only then will the cross become truly wondrous, and we will find true hope in the scars of Christ.

Scars of Sin . . . and Love

Robert Mosher
Graduate Student, Michigan State University (Computer Science);
CAMPUS Missionary

It is certainly worth considering the scars of Christ. Why in His resurrection, when His body was restored to life, were His hands and sides not restored to perfection? Certainly there is a reason. What strikes me when I reflect upon these wounds is "consequences." Though Christ was sinless, He still bears the scars of sin. How far-reaching is the plague of sin that for our wrongdoing, the sinless Son of God should still bear these marks of death? The true cost of sin should give us pause as we live our lives and make decisions. It has been said we crucify Christ anew each time we sin. How can we willfully sin knowing this cost?

Even more, the scars of sin are not born by Christ alone. Though not sinless, the world also suffers for each of our transgressions. Some may be clearly devastating, ruining lives, destroying families, and leading some to start down a dark path. But others may seem more innocent and still have a horrible effect. A few careless words in the church may taint someone's image of Christ. A habit of recklessness may lead to that habit in others, in turn leading to loss of life. The cost of even the smallest sin is too high to ever be indulged in.

Yet Christ's scars serve not only as a reminder of the cost of our sins, but even more so of His choice to bear that cost to save us. Being sinless, he did not need to bear the marks of sin. Nor did the law demand His death. Yet in spite of this, he endured the cross, bearing our sins that it may be seen that God's love for us extends even down to the depths of the grave.

Endnotes

1. E. G. White, *Gospel Workers,* p. 246.

2. CAMPUS, the Center for Adventist Ministry to Public University Students, is a division of the Michigan Conference Public Campus Ministries Department. The office of CAMPUS is based in Ann Arbor, Michigan, near the University of Michigan. The following are the core principles that define the CAMPUS approach to ministry: (1) *Vision:* A Bible-based revival movement in which every student is a missionary; (2) *Methodology:* Biblical simplicity; (3) *Philosophy:* Academic excellence and spiritual excellence; (4) *Goal:* Double our membership every year; (5) *Watchword:* Each one reach one; (6) *Mission:* To prepare secular university campuses for the imminent return of Christ; (7) *Motto:* Taking Higher Education Higher. CAMPUS runs a Missionary Training Program in Ann Arbor, Michigan, near the University of Michigan campus. It is a two-semester, hands-on program that combines sound classroom instruction with practical field training in ministry and outreach activities. The classes are taught by dedicated staff and guest instructors. The goal of the Missionary Training Program is to develop godly and effective leaders, brilliant and winsome soul winners, and sound spiritual counselors for college/university campuses and other professional environments. Limited to no more than a dozen serious students at a time, the program duration overlaps with the academic year at the University of Michigan. For more information, see www.campushope.com.

Chapter 14
SCARRED FOR LIFE

Timothy Treadwell was an American "bear specialist," avid outdoorsman, environmentalist, and documentary film maker. For over 13 years, during summer seasons, he lived peacefully and without weapons among Alaskan grizzly bears. He lived alone with and filmed the bears.

He was exceptionally close to them even though the bears were dangerous. He gave them names, and was often close enough to touch them. He frustrated authorities by refusing to install an electric fence around his camp and refusing to carry bear spray to use as a deterrent.

By 2001, Treadwell became notable enough to receive extensive media attention both on television and in environmental circles. On one occasion when he appeared on a David Letterman's night show, Treadwell described the bears as mostly harmless "party animals."

Two years later, on October 6, 2003, the bodies of Treadwell and his girlfriend were discovered after they were fatally mauled in a bear attack in Katmai National Park in the Alaska Peninsula. Treadwell's disfigured head, partial backbone, and left forearm/hand still wearing his wrist watch were recovered at the scene. His girlfriend's partial remains were also found near the encampment, somewhat buried in a mound of twigs and dirt.

A large male grizzly bear protecting the campsite was killed by park rangers while they attempted to retrieve the bodies. A second adolescent bear was killed a short time later after it charged the park rangers. An investigation revealed human body parts such as fingers and limbs. It is not clear which of these two bears (or which other bear) actually killed the couple. In the 85-year history of Katmai National Park, this was the first incident of a bear killing a person.

The lesson is all too obvious—wild animals cannot be "changed." They are not "mostly harmless party animals." We cannot be cozy with them. Regardless of how comfortable or trusting we may become around these wild animals, sooner or later they will act according to their nature.

To assume otherwise is to flirt with death.

Such is the nature of sin. It is deadly. It has deceived, enslaved, and fatally wounded many.

Sin's Wounds Are Deadly

Sin may initially seem to provide us with some friendly company. We may cuddle with sin, even for a long time, convincing ourselves that we are finding joy or thrill in its bosom. But when it's all over, we discover that sin never lives up to its promise. The pleasures of sin don't last, after all. The Bible says sins' joys are "fleeting pleasures" (Hebrews 11:25). The initial thrill wears off, and the enjoyment inevitably turns to emptiness, misery, shame, and guilt.

Sin will not only lie to us, it also enslaves us. It leads us step-by-by-step through incremental compromises, until it totally controls us. According to Solomon, "The evil deeds of a wicked man ensnare him; *the cords of his sin hold him fast.*"[1] The apostle Peter added his voice: "By what a man is overcome, by this he is enslaved."[2] E. G. White sums it up thus:

> "Sin, however small it may be esteemed, can be indulged in only at the peril of infinite loss. What we do not overcome, will over come us and work out our destruction."[3]

Yes, sin will ultimately destroy us. As surely as the wild bears killed Timothy Treadwell, sin will make prey of those who indulge it. When least expected, the arrows of sin will fatally stab us in the heart. The Word of God says, "The wages of sin is death" (Romans 6:23). And although "there is a way that seems right to a man, but its end is the way of death" (Proverbs 16:25).

Deception, enslavement, and destruction by sin are the wounds that result from our wrong choices. Even when we repent of our sins—and we're forgiven—the consequences of our sins still remain. *The wounds may be healed, but the ugly scars remain.* While God forgives sins, He does not always remove the consequences. Calvary's cross was the penalty for sin, but not necessarily for its consequences. Until Jesus comes again to make all things new, we shall often have to live with the painful consequences of our choices.

And scars from the healed wounds remain with us for a long time.

Healed Wounds, But Ugly Scars was written to help us avoid inflicting wounds upon ourselves—and others. The three sections of the book were intended to show how to avoid needless wounds (Part I), how to obtain healing from our wounds (Part II), and how to live with the ugly scars—after our wounds have been healed (Part III).

Each of these sections highlighted the power of choice. Our choices determine whether or not we inflict wounds upon ourselves and others. They also determine whether or not we shall obtain complete healing from the painful wounds. Finally, our choices affect how we live with the scars after the wounds are healed. Because choices have consequences, we must learn to choose wisely.

In the light of the foregoing pages of this book, we may ask: Where do we go from here? How do we live with the ugly scars that are still with us?

One woman has attempted to provide some answers. Reflecting on her own life in the light of the content of this book, she penned the following reflection. I believe we can learn from her struggles to live with her ugly scars.

The Choice of Turning Toward God

Julia Chappelle-Thomas
Graduate of Grand Valley State University, Michigan
(English) and Editorial Consultant

Where do we go from here (after we've asked for forgiveness and have tried to make amends to those we've wronged)? We look up when we realize we've fallen. We face the consequences with brutal honesty and commit ourselves to making better choices, knowing that we have the chance to turn around when we realize we're going the wrong way.

As I look at myself, as I am today, I see I am covered with so many scars. My loved ones bear scars because of my sins. I grieve over these sins. I cannot change the choices that I've made in the past, and often I seek understanding from others who cannot see beyond my ugly scars. If

I did not know that God has forgiven me and loves me anyway, the despair would be unbearable.

I remember the darkest days of my life, when I distanced myself so far from God that I did not think He could ever love me. Those days are behind me now, by the grace of our loving heavenly Father who never leaves us, no matter what. But because I have walked with God more days of my life than not, even though I've sinned on those same days, I know that I am strong enough to choose Him because I am assured that He still loves me, and I am still His, in spite of my sinful tendencies.

Now that I have grown in faith, I mourn the times I spent separate from my heavenly Father. This is what sin really is: it is a choice to separate our hearts, minds, and actions from God. We are called to seek God's presence, especially when we've sinned:

> Do not fear, for you will not be ashamed;
> Neither be disgraced, for you will not be put to shame;
> For you will forget the shame of your youth,
> And will not remember the reproach of your widowhood anymore.
> For your Maker *is* your husband,
> The LORD of hosts *is* His name;
> And your Redeemer *is* the Holy One of Israel;
> He is called the God of the whole earth.
> For the LORD has called you
> Like a woman forsaken and grieved in spirit,
> Like a youthful wife when you were refused,"
> Says your God (Isaiah 54:4–6).

God calls us to Him at these times to guide us and forgive us, but He also wants us close to Him at these times so that He can assure us that He will love us forever. He still loves us; we are still His. The only thing that can separate us from God and His love for us is our own will to choose. He wants us to choose Him, and He knows that we need to be reminded, especially when we have sinned, that He still loves us and is near. It is only through this blessed assurance that we have what it takes to make better choices! God is with us, and anything is possible with Him and through Him!

We learn to experience joy in the midst of suffering caused by our sin and the sins of others only through God's sustaining love and forgiveness. When we commune with Him by day and by night, we choose Him above all else:

> Seek the LORD while He may be found,
> Call upon Him while He is near.
> Let the wicked forsake his way,
> And the unrighteous man his thoughts;
> Let him return to the LORD,
> And He will have mercy on him;
> And to our God,
> For He will abundantly pardon.
> "For My thoughts are not your thoughts,
> Nor are your ways My ways," says the LORD.
> "For as the heavens are higher than the earth,
> So are My ways higher than your ways,
> And My thoughts than your thoughts" (Isaiah 55: 6–9).

God has promised to forgive our sins when we exercise the free will that He has given us by choosing to walk with Him. In fact, by choosing to walk with him each day, we show that we know that all that we are and all that we have comes from Him: not by our feeble hands but through Him only.

Because God loves us so perfectly and completely, we are able to love ourselves and to love others as ourselves. Only through God's grace are we strong enough to conquer our sinful tendencies and desires. We need Him to guide us each day in our relationships with others; we can only turn away from sin by turning toward Him.

Because He sent His Son to pay our debt of sin on the cross, we have the strength to deal with the consequences of our sins. He is present when we lash out at those who have hurt us in retaliation; He is present when we take that which is not ours; He is present when we are unfaithful to those with whom we have bound our lives by commitment; and He is there when we harm ourselves by taking risks or participate in self-destructive acts.

We will experience the pain of our sins; there is no escape from it. Those against whom we have sinned may not forgive us for a very long time and, regretfully, in some cases, they may not forgive us at all. In that way, their sin divides them from us, but it also separates them from God, who calls us all to forgive one another. God knows our hearts, and He comforts us when we experience the consequences of our sin. He gives us hope for a better day, the strength to keep trying and to keep forgiving others, and the awareness that He is with us, always. Sin divides us from our loved ones and from ourselves, but if we do not seek God because of our sin, we sin twice.

He is with us, always. He calls us in a quiet voice, but we can hear Him above the din of humanity, if we seek Him. He is always there! We are His people. He bought us with the blood of His Son, and through Christ we come to Him. Heed His call to us from the Word of God:

> Arise, shine;
> For your light has come!
> And the glory of the LORD is risen upon you.
> For behold, the darkness shall cover the earth,
> And deep darkness the people;
> But the LORD will arise over you,
> And His glory will be seen upon you.
> The Gentiles shall come to your light,
> And kings to the brightness of your rising (Isaiah 60: 1-3).

This is His call to action for His people: every day, choose to be at one with Him, no matter what. He made us in His image, but He made us free moral agents, also, so that we would be capable of choosing Him. If, and when you fall, He waits for you to go to Him and to acknowledge that He is your God. He will remind you, "You are *still* mine."

Scarred for A Moment

In the above reflection, Julia speaks for many of us who bear the scars of our past and are struggling with how to live with them. None of us can escape the fact that for our entire earthly lives we shall carry those scars. They will remain as long as we live. They will serve as reminders of the choices that we—and others—have made.

Regrettably, some of the scars were the result of self-inflicted wounds. We brought them upon ourselves by the choices we have made. But we wear many other scars because of the choices and actions of others—a drunk driver, an accident at our workplace, the divorce in our home, the violation of our innocence, and unjust practices in our institutions.

But even with these wounds inflicted by others, we have often made them worse by our lack of forgiving spirit. The most ugly scars are those resulting from our unforgiving spirit.

Regardless of the cause of our scars, we can rejoice in the fact that all our earthly scars are there for a limited period of time only. We are scarred for a moment. We shall only carry them for the remainder of our pilgrimage on earth. Our scars will no longer remain when Jesus comes again to give us our new, glorious bodies.

> For our citizenship is in heaven, from which we also eagerly wait for the Savior, the Lord Jesus Christ, who will transform our lowly [scarred] body that it may be conformed to His glorious body, according to the working by which He is able even to subdue all things to Himself (Philippians 3:20, 21).

This thought of Christ's glorious return to give us scar-free bodies—and mind and spirit—was that which sustained the Old Testament patriarch Job in the midst of his own struggle with pain and afflictions:

> For I know that my Redeemer lives,
> And He shall stand at last on the earth;
> And after my skin is destroyed, this I know,
> That in my flesh I shall see God . . . (Job 19:25, 26).

Yes, although we wear our scars today, it is only for a moment. When Christ comes again to give us our glorious bodies, there will be no more scars. All the vestiges of pain and death will be replaced:

> Behold, I tell you a mystery: We shall not all sleep, but we shall all be changed—in a moment, in the twinkling of an eye, at the last trumpet. For the trumpet will sound, and the dead will be raised incorruptible [un-scarred], and we shall be changed. For this corruptible [scarred] must put on incorruption [un-scarred], and this mortal must put on immortality. So when this corruptible [scarred] has put on incorruption [un-scarred], and this mortal has put on immortality, then shall be brought to pass the saying that is written: "Death is swallowed up in victory." "O Death, where is your sting? O Hades, where is your victory?" (1 Corinthians 15:51-55).

Our scars today are only for a moment. For when Christ comes again, all the reminders of our painful wounds—the ugly scars—will be gone forever. He would heal us of all the lingering ugly scars.

Not so, however, with our Lord Himself. He is scarred forever!

Scarred Forever!

Unlike our scars which are for a moment, Christ's glorious body will forever bear the scars from the wounds He sustained while on earth. The glorious body of our resurrected Lord on Easter Sunday still bore the scars from the wounds inflicted on Good Friday. And for all eternity He will bear those His scars.

But why would our scars be healed, while His would remain? Was it because He wasn't able to heal His own wounds? We know He was—and is—able to heal. For while He was here on earth, our Lord demonstrated His power to heal. He healed the brokenhearted, set the captives free, made the lame to walk again, and helped the blind to see! Since He was able to heal, He surely could have erased the scars from His resurrected body.

Also, since our Lord could—and can—forgive sin, He surely could have removed the marks of sin from His own glorious body. The God who could raise Jesus from the dead, could have surely performed a divine cosmetic surgery and given His Son a scar-free body.

So the question is, Why does Christ's glorious body still carry the marks, while our glorious bodies will be scar-free when He comes again? Three answers come readily to mind. In these answers we find some motivations to live today with our ugly scars.

1. Christ's eternal scars are proof that He is real. You will remember after His resurrection, our Lord urged Thomas, "Reach your finger here, and look at My hands; and reach your hand here, and put it into My side. Do not be unbelieving, but believing" (John 20:27). The scars were evidence that Jesus was who He claimed to be.

If there's anyone out there still doubting the reality of God, they need no other proof. They should look at the scars of Christ and believe.

2. The eternal scars of Christ are proof of His love and forgiveness. They remind us that Jesus paid the price for us. "He was *wounded for our transgressions,* He was *bruised for our iniquities;* the chastisement for our peace was upon Him, and *by His stripes we are healed*" (Isaiah 53:5).

Whereas our scars are for a moment (they will be effaced when our Lord comes again), Christ's scars will be forever as a constant reminder of His love and forgiveness. Our sins are forgiven because of the fatal wounds He sustained. Writes E. G. White:

> Christ was treated as we deserve, that we might be treated as He deserves. He was condemned for our sins, in which He had no share, that we might be justified by His righteousness, in which we had no share. He suffered the death which was ours, that we might receive the life which was His. "*With His stripes we are healed*" (*The Desire of Ages,* p. 25).

3. The eternal scars of Christ demonstrate His identification with the human family. He bears the scars to assure us that He knows our human frailty because He Himself partook of the same. He understands human pain and suffering. He knows by experience what it means to be abandoned, betrayed, and forsaken.

The scars forever remind us that in all our afflictions He is afflicted (Isa 63:9). He knows what it means to suffer. So He can help us in our suffering, thus enabling us to move on, despite our scars.

> Therefore, since we have a great high priest who has gone through the heavens, Jesus the Son of God, let us hold firmly to the faith we profess. For we do not have a high priest who is unable to sympathize with our weaknesses, but we have one who has been tempted in every way, just as we are—yet was without sin. Let us then approach the throne of grace with confidence, so that we may receive mercy and find grace to help us in our time of need (Hebrews 4:14-16).

As I pointed out in the introduction to this book, only a Risen Savior with scars can understand our scarred hearts. Today, He is our Mediator in heaven, working to heal us of all our wounds:

> The Elder Brother of our race is by the eternal throne. He looks upon every soul who is turning his face toward Him as the Savior. He knows the weaknesses of humanity, what we want, and where the strength of our temptations lie by experience; for He was in all points tempted as we are, yet without sin. He is watching over you, trembling child of God. Are you tempted? He will deliver. Are you weak? He will strengthen. Are you ignorant? He will enlighten. *Are you wounded? He will heal.* The Lord `telleth the number of the stars;' and yet `He healeth the broken in heart, and bindeth up their wounds.' Ps. 147:4, 3. `Come unto Me,' is His invitation. Whatever your anxieties and trials, spread out your case before the Lord. Your spirit will be braced for endurance. The way will be opened for you to disentangle yourself from embarrassment and difficulty. The weaker and

> more helpless you know yourself to be, the stronger will you become in His strength. The heavier your burdens, the more blessed the rest in casting them upon the Burden Bearer.[4]

We may be scarred for life—that is, for the remainder of our earthly existence on earth. But He is scarred for all eternity. Our scars are for a moment. His scars are forever. Let's bear these facts in mind when we are struggling with our ugly scars today.

When, on account of our ugly scars, we are tempted to doubt His existence or reality in our lives, His eternal scars assure us that He is there for us. When, because of the load of our ugly scars, we chafe under the burden of guilt and shame, His eternal scars assure us of His forgiveness and constant love. And when our ugly scars make us think nobody knows what we're going through, Christ's eternal scars should encourage us that He forever identifies with us.

In view of these facts, we can today live at peace with our ugly scars. Yes, we may have to live with the painful consequences of our choices—and those of others. But Jesus will come again. And He will once and for all remove every scar:

Our Lord Jesus Christ Himself has promised:

> "Let not your heart be troubled; you believe in God, believe also in Me. In My Father's house are many mansions; if it were not so, I would have told you. I go to prepare a place for you. And if I go and prepare a place for you, I will come again and receive you to Myself; that where I am, there you may be also (John 14:1-3).

The apostle Paul assures us:

> For the Lord Himself will descend from heaven with a shout, with the voice of an archangel, and with the trumpet of God. And the dead in Christ will rise first. Then we who are alive and remain shall be caught up together with them in the clouds to meet the Lord in the air. And thus we shall always be with the Lord (1 Thessalonians 4:16-17).

And John, the beloved apostle, reports what our Lord Jesus Christ revealed to him in vision:

> Now I saw a new heaven and a new earth, for the first heaven and the first earth had passed away. . . . And God will wipe away every tear from their eyes; there shall be no more death, nor sorrow, nor crying. There shall be no more pain, for the former things have passed away . . . And He said to me, "Write, for these words are true and faithful" (Revelation 21:1-5).

Endnoes

1. Proverbs 5:22; NIV.
2. 2 Peter 2:19; NASB.
3. E. G. White, *Steps to Christ,* p. 32-33.
4. E. G. White, *The Desire of Ages,* p. 329.

RECOMMENDED READING

If *Healed Wounds, But Ugly Scars* has been a blessing to you, you will also greatly appreciate some of the other insightful books by the author. (Information about how to obtain them is found at the end of this section.)

AUTHOR'S BOOK ON TRIALS AND AFFLICTIONS

In the journey through life, trials await us all. For at one point or another, every one of us is bound to experience the agony of pain, disappointment, sorrow, hurt, loss, or some other form of suffering that will severely test our resiliency and character. We may also suffer afflictions—prolonged ordeals of suffering that lie deeper in the soul. God uses these trials and afflictions to cultivate in us the virtue of patience.

You can tell that the Lord is developing patience in you when you run into many anguishing experiences; when the things or people you depend on suddenly fail you; when your life seems to be in detours; when prolonged illness and other forms of affliction plague you; when your situation in life goes from bad to worse. Above all, you know you are being schooled in patience when you cry out to God for help, and He doesn't seem to hear or care.

Patience in the Midst of Trials and Afflictions insightfully explains the nature of patience, why God permits trials and afflictions, and how you can benefit from them. This life-changing book will be a source of encouragement to you and your loved ones. It will give you confidence in God's guidance and renew your determination to trust Him, no matter what.

ISBN: 1-890014-04-4. Price: $10.99

AUTHOR'S BOOK ON LOVE

Love. It's the never-ending, driving quest—the all-consuming need—the motivating desire—of every man, woman, and child on earth.

But just what is love? Is it accurately defined by the sum total of all the song lyrics, love poems, and love stories ever written? All the movies ever filmed? All the dramas ever acted?

Toward a deeper, more satisfying answer to the question "What is love?" the This Is Love book manuscript contains a distilled, carefully chosen sampling of poems, quotations, articles and essays, stories, and personal reflections focused on love.

Some of the material in these pages is original to the author. Some represents the best thoughts of other writers. Found here are the words of those divinely inspired and those who have simply shared their own ideas. But in a search for the true definition of love, where this This Is Love book best succeeds is in its undeviating focus on the Source of all real love—the One whose name is synonymous with love.

Real love cannot exist outside of a relationship. And whether ours is horizontal, involving other people around us—or vertical, between us and our God—or both, this book will open new vistas of understanding and delight as readers take in its pages.

ISBN: 978-890014-11-7. Price $12.99

AUTHOR'S BOOK ON INTEGRITY

Not For Sale is a call to daily self-examination—and action. It highlights the consequences of the cowardly silence all too often displayed by some otherwise good and well-meaning people.

Contending that silence, neutrality, or indifference in times of crisis is a criminal act, if not a betrayal of faith, this book makes an urgent plea against choosing to do nothing in the face of wrong-doing. It's a thoughtful yet impassioned appeal to rediscover the strength and power of integrity and principle.

This volume challenges men and women—especially those with the energy and idealism of youth—to claim the moral high ground in their lives. The character crisis cries out for those who cannot be silenced by fear, threat or intimidation. It cries out for those who cannot be lured to cowardice or compromise by blandishments of money, prestige, or power. It cries out for those who will stand boldly—and state emphatically—that they are Not For Sale.

Hardcover: ISBN: 978-1890014-09-4. Price $17.99

For these and other resources contact your local Christian Book Center, ABC (www.adventistbookcenter.com) or:

Berean Books,
P. O. Box 2799,
Ann Arbor, MI 48197.
Tel. 1-800-423-1319.
www.berean-books.org

For quantity discounts to churches, schools, or groups, contact the author at the above address or at: Phone: 734-528-2863; FAX: 734-528-2869; E-mail: skpipim@gmail.com.